PHOENIX AT COVENTRY

PHOENIX AT COVENTRY

THE BUILDING OF A CATHEDRAL

BASIL SPENCE

HARPER & ROW, PUBLISHERS, NEW YORK AND EVANSTON

*Printed in Great Britain
for Harper & Row, Publishers, Incorporated*

1. *In the shadow of the entrance porch looking up at one of the two crosses which are set between its columns.*

TO JOAN

FOREWORD BY THE BISHOP OF COVENTRY

MY FIRST reaction after receiving the invitation to become the fifth Bishop of Coventry was one of profound gratitude. I realised that I was one of the luckiest men in the Church of England. It is indeed a privilege to be associated closely with the construction and preparation for use of a new Cathedral.

Within a few days, I had the privilege of meeting Professor Basil Spence and found that here was a man inspired—a man with an ardent, glowing faith in God—who believed in his vocation to build a Cathedral expressive of the Christian Faith in contemporary terms.

In the course of the past six years this, my first impression, has deepened and matured. Basil Spence is a prophet who seeks to proclaim the Word of God in terms that a modern generation can understand. Like all great artists he hates the shoddy, the sentimental, the second-rate. 'Only the very best will do for God' is his motto. With this in mind he approached some of the greatest contemporary artists—men who with courage and determination are in the advance guard of modern art.

Some may think that Basil Spence is a revolutionary. In certain respects he is, but it is even more true to say that he is an evolutionary —one who builds solidly upon past foundations, who seeks to integrate his modern ideas into the experience of past traditions. He builds on the past, learns from the past, seeks to mould the past into a creative and courageous present.

As he shows in his book, he had the conception of a Cathedral built around the High Altar. The light from the windows focuses upon this great Altar—the central meeting-point around which congregations offer their worship to God and at which congregations receive their food from God.

Basil Spence has very clear-cut ideas as to what a Cathedral is for —essentially and primarily it is for worship, and to this end nobody must be prevented from entering into this worship by pillars which obscure. In his Cathedral every person has an uninterrupted view of the Altar. But to his mind a Cathedral must not merely be a place of worship apart from life, rather must worship by the offering of all life to God. Therefore his Cathedral has a great deal of plain glass through which the light and the influences, the tensions and the aspirations of the surrounding community can enter and find their purpose in the offering of all that is worthy to God.

This Cathedral is set in the very midst of the teeming, industrial and commercial life of the City of Coventry, not something apart from life on the circumference but rather placed at the very heart and kernel of life's activities, drawing them up through its worship and liturgy to God's very Throne.

A Cathedral must build bridges to the surrounding community, one of the bridges being through the Chapel of Unity in which men of different religious denominations can meet, think together, pray together, be silent together, study together, understand one another's ways of worship and go out together into the common service of mankind. Another bridge is contained in the Chapel of Industry—the Chapel of Christ the Servant. Here men and women from Industry and Commerce can gather to pray for their work, to offer their work to the Almighty. Yet a third avenue of communication is through the adjacent ruins of the ancient Cathedral—ever standing to remind men of the tragedy of war, the overruling purposes of God. As a man inspired he had the foresight to leave these ruins and to build the Cathedral at right-angles to them, bearing in

Foreword

mind that both the ancient and the modern Cathedrals—expressive of the crucified and the risen Christ—would form together one Cathedral with one spire and one purpose.

It has been an honour and a source of inspiration to work alongside this great artist, a man who never rests content with his work but is always striving, thinking and planning to improve it, ever seeking new ways through which to express his glowing faith.

It is my hope that this book will be read by many and that all who read it will be urged to visit this Cathedral, to send it forward on its long journey with their prayers and their encouragement.

CUTHBERT COVENTRY

MY gratitude goes to: my publisher Jocelyn Gibb for his Job-like patience; to his reader Celia Ramsey for optimism, courage and hard work in attempting to teach me English grammar and something about that mystery, literary form; to Anthony Blee (helped by Johanna) for designing the cover and helping with the presentation; to Henk Snoek, Alfred Cracknell, Hugo de Burgh Galwey and Mrs. Porter for the photographs and to my daughter Gillian Blee, Elizabeth Mather and Jillian Collins for typing the manuscript over and over again.

B. S.

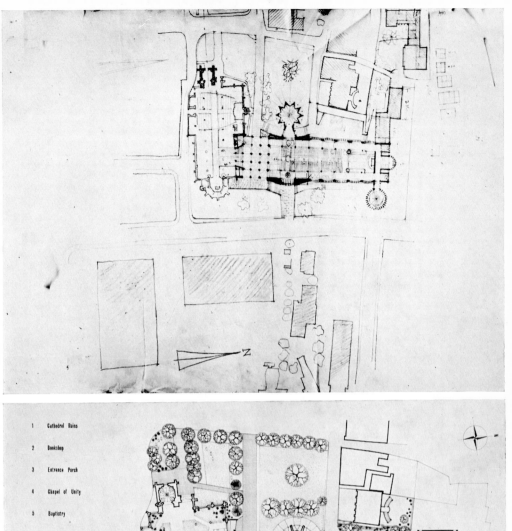

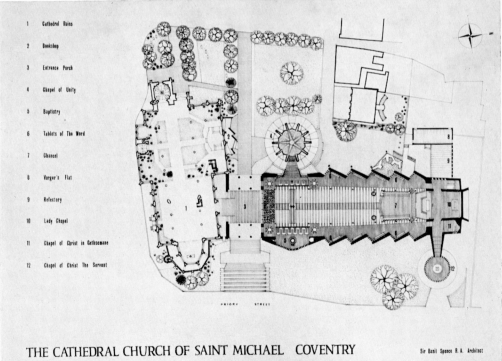

1	Cathedral Ruins
2	Bookshop
3	Entrance Porch
4	Chapel of Unity
5	Baptistry
6	Tablets of The Word
7	Chancel
8	Verger's Flat
9	Refectory
10	Lady Chapel
11	Chapel of Christ in Gethsemane
12	Chapel of Christ The Servant

PRIORY STREET

THE CATHEDRAL CHURCH OF SAINT MICHAEL COVENTRY

Sir Basil Spence R.A. Architect

2 and 3. (Above) *The very first sketch plan, drawn immediately after Basil Spence's first visit to the site. The characteristic zig-zag wall formation has not yet emerged, but it bears (below) a remarkable resemblance to the plan of the finished building.*

CHAPTERS

CONTENTS

ILLUSTRATIONS

Illustrations

* Colour plates.   [1]*Henk Snoek.*   [2] *The Author.*

Only a fool will build in defiance of the past. What is new and significant always must be grafted to old roots, the truly vital roots that are chosen with great care from the ones that merely survive. And what a slow and delicate process it is to distinguish radical vitality from the wastes of mere survival, but that is the only way to achieve progress instead of disaster.

BARTOK

CHAPTER 1

The Conception

ON D plus 2, June 1944, I was dug in just off the beaches of Normandy. An Army friend, Laurie Paynter, also dug into the ground for protection, asked me just before we fell asleep what my ambition was. The circumstances were such as to set one thinking about such mortal longings. I said, 'To build a cathedral.'

This remark was perhaps prompted by an incident I had witnessed that day. At Oustreham and Hermanville, in the Sword Sector where I had landed, are two beautiful Norman churches. The Germans had placed snipers in each church tower, and in order to winkle them out tanks were brought up which blasted away at the belfry windows. As an architect witnessing the murder of a beautiful building, I felt that other ways should have been found to remove those snipers, for I firmly believe that the creative genius of man, the spark of life that he carries while on earth, is manifest in his efforts, and that once this is lost through the destruction of great works, the world is the poorer, for that particular light has been put out for ever.

Later that year in Brussels I read in an English newspaper that Sir Giles Gilbert Scott, the creator of that magnificent Anglican cathedral at Liverpool, had produced a design for the New Coventry Cathedral, and my mind went back to 15th November 1940, when as a Staff Captain (Intelligence) I had reported the Coventry Raid to my General. I remembered telling him that the Cathedral had been destroyed in the night, the first of many as we thought, but as

I

things turned out the only one to be completely gutted. I remembered the feeling of irretrievable loss, wondering how it could be replaced, and thinking what a challenge it would be to our generation should it ever be rebuilt.

The first great church in Coventry was started in 1043 by Lady Godiva and the Earl Leofric—a magnificent building of great length and importance. Remains of the West Front can be seen today and we discovered a fragment of the east apse during the construction of the new Cathedral; indeed we built one wall of the Cathedral on these remains, which connected Godiva's Cathedral with the perpendicular church destroyed by Hitler's bombs on 14th November 1940. Godiva's great Abbey church fell a victim to Henry the Eighth's decree, which dissolved many of our monasteries, and it was pulled down and used as a quarry about 1539.

The second Cathedral, originally a parish church and raised to the status of a Cathedral only in 1918, was completed in 1433, about four hundred years after the first Great Church (it was almost 500 years later that Hitler's fire bombs destroyed the second Cathedral). Out of these ruins rises the third Christian temple—a Phoenix from the Ashes.

Coventry's Cathedrals have always had a turbulent history, and Sir Giles Scott's 1944 design was not accepted by the Royal Fine Arts Commission. Conflicting requirements of the clergy made impossible demands on the architect and Sir Giles resigned in 1947.

Then the Harlech Commission was set up; in 1947 it produced a report recommending that a new Cathedral should be built on the site of the old and that an open architectural competition should be organised with the condition that the design should be in the 'Gothic style'—a condition which was later discarded.

The Commission also recommended that a Reconstruction Committee should be appointed, composed of lay and clergy, to work with the selected architect in the construction of the new Cathedral. The finances were to come mainly from the War Damage Commission, who would supply funds for a 'plain replacement'.

In June 1950 the competition conditions for a new Cathedral were issued. (See Appendix B, page 109.) It was open to any architect in the British Commonwealth, but it also included architects in the Republic of Ireland.

I remember vividly the effect this had on me: here was the opportunity I had never thought would come in these materialistic days when new cathedrals are so seldom built. Since the end of the war the only real work I could get was the design of exhibitions; I had been concerned with practically all the major ones since 1945, when I had been appointed Chief Architect for 'Britain Can Make It'. In 1950 I was heavily committed with the 'Festival of Britain'.

I found this work interesting, exciting and lucrative, but I was becoming known as an 'exhibition architect' and my real interest lay in 'solid work'. The ephemeral character of exhibitions which, at their best, are only a form of architectural journalism, did not appeal to me and I was seriously thinking of throwing everything up and going to America when the competition was announced.

I sent for the conditions.

They were extremely well framed, calculated to stimulate the imagination and kindle the enthusiasm. The first page contained a message from the Bishop and Provost:

'The Cathedral is to speak to us and to generations to come of the Majesty, the Eternity and the Glory of God. God, therefore, direct you.

'It is a Cathedral of the Church of England. In terms of function, what should such a Cathedral express? It stands as a witness to the central dogmatic truths of the Christian Faith. Architecturally it should seize on those truths and thrust them upon the man who comes in from the street.

'The doctrine and the worship of the Church of England is liturgically centred in the Eucharist. The Cathedral should be built to enshrine the altar. This should be the ideal of the architect, not to conceive a building and to place in it an altar, but to conceive an altar and to create a building.

'In the Anglican liturgy it is the people's altar; the altar should gather the people, it should offer access for worship and invitation to Communion.

'With the altar—in the unity of worship—there is the preaching of the Gospel among our people of Coventry and the interpretation of the Word.

'The theology of the Cathedral we put before you to direct your thought. Prayer will be with you from the Cathedral Crypt and from the Diocese of Coventry. May God be with you in this great matter.'

The Cathedral could be in any style; it could face any direction, as east–west orientation was not considered essential; it must seat 1,650 people, provide a Lady Chapel, a Children's Chapel, a Guild Chapel and a Chapel of the Resurrection for private prayer. This was all fairly normal, but the requirement for a Chapel of Unity came as a surprise.

A Chapel of Unity was a strange requirement for a Cathedral. It was completely without precedent and would therefore require close study. The Chapel would be administered by a joint Council of Anglican and Free Churchmen, its purpose is Joint Worship, its final objective Christian Unity. I was stimulated by this idea and felt it was capable of strong architectural expression.

Another unusual condition was the provision of a Christian

4

Service Centre, a kind of Community Centre with a large meeting room with a kitchen, a library and Committee rooms.

One of the most important factors governing a competition is the judging of it. For Coventry the President of the Royal Institute of British Architects had recommended a Jury of three eminent architects—Sir Percy Thomas, Sir Howard Robertson and Sir Edward Maufe—all acknowledged champions of young architects and the last a competition winner for Guildford Cathedral. I think it was the knowledge of such fair judgement as well as the opportunity itself that encouraged over 600 architects to apply for the Conditions, but the problem was such a difficult one that only 219 made the final submission and were judged. Even so, I was told that if all the drawings were put end to end they would have stretched the length of Princes Street, Edinburgh. The entries set a formidable task for the judges, for this was one of the best supported competitions ever organised, with entries received from all corners of the Commonwealth.

I was living in Edinburgh then and my main office was there; so one dull day in October, with no sunshine to brighten the autumn afternoon, my wife and I got into my car and went straight to Coventry. This first visit to the ruined Cathedral was one of the most deeply stirring and moving days I have ever spent.

The bombed Cathedral still had its fine, graceful tower and spire intact, but all that remained of the Cathedral walls was a lace-like screen of masonry, buttresses and pinnacles with perpendicular windows without glass, some with the tracery still there, but others gaping wide.

As soon as I set foot on the ruined nave I felt the impact of delicate enclosure. It was still a cathedral. Instead of the beautiful wooden roof it had the skies as a vault. This was a Holy Place, and although the Conditions specified that we need keep only the tower, spire, and the two crypt chapels, I felt I could not destroy this beautiful place, and that whatever else I did, I would preserve as much of the old Cathedral as I could.

This feeling of reverence was intensified as we walked to the Stone Altar (made from the stones that had fallen inwards after the destruction) and the Charred Cross constructed from roof timbers not quite burnt out, on the altar of the Cross of Nails and behind it the words 'Father Forgive'.

I was deeply moved. I saw the old Cathedral as standing clearly for the Sacrifice, one side of the Christian Faith, and I knew my task was to design a new one which should stand for the Triumph of the Resurrection.

We moved to the North and looked out through the glassless tracery over the ground reserved for the New Cathedral, over Saint Michael's Avenue, the gravestones, trees and bombed houses, and in my mind's eye I got one of those pictures that architects sometimes get. This one, however, was unusually clear—a great nave and an altar that was an invitation to Communion, and a huge picture behind it. But, as always with mind pictures, it was ever changing. I could not see the altar clearly but through the bodies of the Saints.

In these few moments the idea of the design was planted. In essence it has never changed.

CHAPTER 2

The Ground is Prepared

I WAS BORN in India and when I was eight years old my father took me to see the caves at Elephanta, just outside Bombay.

This was the first architectural experience of my life and it is still vivid. The vast chambers carved out of solid rock, rich in sculpture and intricate detail, gave a tremendous feeling of size; the cool temperature inside contrasted with the heat outside, and the dim lighting revealed features of the interior only after the eye had got used to darkness.

Perhaps I would be disappointed if I returned to these caves with their ancient carvings, for I believe that only in one's imagination can there be perfection. There is no perfection in reality, for it always holds something that jars on the picture carried in the mind's eye.

The feeling of awe and timelessness that was so strong in the caves at Elephanta was revived when I visited those remarkable painted caves in Lascaux in the centre of France; I felt the same mystery, and the knowledge that strange ceremonies must have taken place in these early temples. This sense of ancient rites recurred when I visited Delphi in Greece and Zimbabwe in Rhodesia.

My second important architectural experience was in Easter 1927 when, as a second-year student of Architecture, I visited Yorkshire on a sketching tour. I was alone and entered York Minster through the southern porch. Shafts of the morning light shot the Gothic mouldings with ruby and gold. The choir was practising for the Easter services, the organ adding lustre to the richness of boys' voices and the impact on me of the Five Sisters' window was tremendous. I realised for the first time that architecture could have a deep spiritual significance, and I knew that my life as an architect would be incomplete if I never had the opportunity to build a Cathedral. With the idealism of youth I felt certain that architecture could rise to greatness if its goal was Faith.

My third fundamental architectural experience was the realisation of England's wealth in places of worship built during the Middle Ages, and after my first visit to York I spent practically every holiday and every spare moment as a student measuring and sketching churches all over England and also in Scotland. The abundance of Gothic parish churches in Northamptonshire; the Nene Valley with its spires; King's College Chapel, Cambridge, which to me is one of the most beautiful temples in Britain; the colour and beauty of the East Anglian churches. I realised that in England there existed a tradition of vitality and integrity, and that in my drawings I was recording the history of contemporary English architecture.

I realised too that in these churches was embodied a great truth: that architecture should grow out of the conditions of the time, should not be a copy of past styles, and must be a clear expression of belief in contemporary thought. This I saw as our heritage, for we are an inventive nation and it is a denial of a natural characteristic to limit our architectural vocabulary to past forms. In fact, I began to believe that it is the duty of the architect not to copy, but to think afresh.

I already knew that some of our big cathedrals display a whole history of mediaeval architecture, each period clearly stated with little repetition except in principle. Yet cathedrals like Gloucester, Canterbury and Ely, which house many hundred of years of architectural thinking, still have an essential unity; but, what is more remarkable, do not surrender their vitality and integrity.

The Ground is Prepared

Gloucester impressed me greatly, for here we see a beautiful nave, strong and robust, in the best Norman tradition, with heavy nave pillars and small windows and at the east end, where the chancel was rebuilt in the Perpendicular period, a great contrast. This chancel and its east window is a memorial to the men who fell in the Battle of Crécy, and the great sheet of glass, beautiful in mediaeval colours, is perhaps the first glass wall to be created in England.

What an example it is to modern architects, especially as the stone-masons did not have the advantage of engineering techniques of extruded metals and reinforced or pre-stressed concrete or steel; they simply placed stone on stone. This east window has withstood all ravages and looks perhaps more beautiful today, with the gentle weathering of time, than when it was first erected.

Gloucester, with its surge of organic growth, starts with the strong stem of the nave and blossoms into the beautiful flower of the great east window. Yet this building, built in two contemporary styles, has an amazing unity, and the climax round the altar is to my mind an architectural masterpiece.

I began to ask myself, how is it that unity can be achieved with two such divergent styles? We see practically the same thing in Ely, where there is a Norman nave and decorated choir but also one of the most interesting and daring crossings of nave and transept in English church architecture—the crossing which was such an inspiration to Sir Christopher Wren when he came to design the dome of St. Paul's.

How is it, I wondered, that advocates of our national architecture consider a contemporary style to be completely wrong when applied to churches, when it is clear that the whole character of our churches in the past has depended on integrity and a sense of adventure from which sprang our native architecture?

Many sincere people, little realising that our tradition is such an

adventurous one, are shocked when architects think in this traditional way; they cannot see that the true traditionalists are people
who think simply in their own era. The copyists, then, are surely the
revolutionaries.

But how to achieve this unity, so evident in all our great churches?
After some thought I felt certain there existed a common blood
group, a family likeness that springs from common parenthood and
a rhythmic consistency. All the churches most successfully developed
are those that have been added to in the same material or a material
that is in sympathy with the original. When an historic building is to
be extended it is a trained instinct to be kind to the old structure, not
to destroy its voice, to encourage growth and not to wipe out and
start again. That is what is important. All great buildings show a
rhythmic consistency, even though they may contain four or five contemporary styles each showing integrity. This conception, after all,
can be accepted because the church stands for permanence, continuity and vitality—a living Faith.

CHAPTER 3

The Idea

IT IS TRUE to say that the idea-seed established in my mind during the first five minutes of our visit to Coventry grew like a plant and I never considered an alternative; although in a normal project alternatives and variations are very much the rule. The design developed gradually, almost by itself, but the essential idea remained. On my return to Edinburgh from Coventry and within the next twenty-four hours I did my first plan (which is shown facing page xii) and the main parts of it are unaltered today.

I had determined to keep practically the whole of the old Cathedral, the new one growing out of it and being incomplete without it. On the plan I placed the altar in the north, and a porch connected the old and the new buildings.

I saw the Chapel of Unity as a star, for a star is a strong shape and being a regular figure it gave me the sense of unity and strength. I felt it should be dominant and separate; I put it on the axis of the font, as there were to be two main axes—from the old Cathedral to the altar and from the Chapel of Unity to the font.

The porch, which had a glass division between it and the new Cathedral, strode over Saint Michael's Avenue. On the glass screen, which on the original design could be lowered into the ground, the Saints were engraved.

I was strongly influenced by the Cathedral at Albi, for although I visited this wonderful church in the South of France only after the competition, I already knew it well from plans and photographs.

The walls rise sheer and though the exterior is plain and simple it has a grandeur in strong contrast to the interior, which is very rich. The same is true of S. Apollinare-in-Classe at Ravenna; the exterior is a quiet invitation to enter but the impact of the interior is staggering. Outside simple brick, inside marble and mosaic with a half dome of glorious mosaic over the High Altar. These churches turn a casual visitor into a worshipper—here is architecture that functions.

I therefore planned a very simple exterior of pinky-grey stone similar to the original Cathedral and a rich interior with a huge tapestry behind the High Altar.

On my first plans the bays of the Cathedral walls were curved to give a feeling of great niches on the interior, with stained-glass windows in these niches. Now the walls are 'zig-zagged'. How this came about is a curious story.

I was working extremely hard during the winter of 1950. The Festival of Britain with which I was engaged had many crises and I was working late every night on the Cathedral designs after my day's normal work. I found solace and contentment working quietly on the design between 9 o'clock in the evening and into the early morning. The competition was a testing time for me for several reasons, and as usual in periods of stress and overwork, something went bad—I got an abscess on one of my upper teeth.

My dentist advised immediate extraction with a local anaesthetic. I hate injections and at best I feel queer, but now I was run down and exhausted and I passed out.

My dream was wonderful. I was walking through the Cathedral and it looked marvellous, with a light like Chartres. The altar looked tremendous, backed by a huge tapestry, but I could not see the windows until I went right in and turned half back—the walls were zig-zagged!

The Idea

When I came to (I had been 'out' for quite a few minutes; the dentist had perspiration pouring from his brow) I told him of my dream. All he said was, 'I will send in a bill for that idea.'

I can truly say I had not considered using this type of wall before I saw it in this dream. Of course, it may have been at the back of my mind, for the zig-zag is a well-known way of directional lighting. It certainly fitted in with the plan, as the windows would then face south-east and south-west; the coloured shafts of light would streak to the altar.

Even though I was determined to have a very simple exterior, and I did not want to copy any of the Gothic architectural vocabulary such as buttresses, pinnacles and pointed arches, I felt there must be continuity and unity with the old. I knew that the accepted way of being *avant-garde* is consciously to avoid anything that even reminds one of the past. I had done this in the exhibitions, and the Sea and Ships Pavilion in the South Bank was an example of this way of thinking. The object of an exhibition is to excite and even shock, above all to tell some story quickly and fully. I felt that the object of a Cathedral Church was very different. There must be continuity, unity and permanence as well as that vital ingredient—vitality. I was therefore interested in links existing between my way of thinking and the old, and if any element did not contribute to the concept I believed in, I pitched it out ruthlessly.

By the time I designed the Sea and Ships Pavilion I was bored with the stretched glass skin over a frame, and I was much more interested in the plastic expression of a natural material like stone. For the Cathedral I would not have a frame; I would have a solid building standing on its own feet, four solid walls and a roof.

The simplicity of the idea appealed to me and the possibility of walking this aesthetic 'tight-rope' I found exhilarating. I would have a punctured stone wall of great simplicity enclosing the altar.

I would have a vault, I would have aisles, stained glass, a marble floor, a great tapestry, choir stalls. The Cathedral would be like a plain jewel-casket with many jewels inside: but the biggest and brightest jewel would be the Altar. I would have the same acoustic properties in my building as the great cathedrals, it would sound like the old cathedrals during Matins and Evensong. I would not ventilate, and with luck it would even smell like an old one. But I still had to tackle the question of unity with the existing building.

I found that two separate rhythms existed in the old Cathedral, the big rhythm created by the spacing of the nave pillars and the small one made by the spacing of mullions in the perpendicular tracery. I took these two rhythms and made them into my 'blood groups' for the new building. I pursued this course relentlessly; the plan worked out mathematically using these two modules. I had already decided to use a stone of great beauty similar to the old.

The stage was set.

From now on the plan required fresh thinking. I would not use mouldings in my stone-work as these delicate and beautiful forms, so characteristic of the old buildings I had measured, were a direct outcome of the conditions of labour existing when the old cathedrals were built. The hammer and chisel were the tools of the craftsman; now we had frame and carborundum saws, so I designed all the stone forms round these tools. The baptistry window is a child of these parents.

The nave windows, too, were designed in this way with chunky bands of crystalline masonry. My mullions were deep diamond-shaped 'louvres', much deeper than the old, but the spacing was the same, giving a reasonable working unit for the stained-glass artist.

The idea for the vault came slowly, developed gradually and has only recently been finalised. On the competition drawings it was entirely of concrete in great plastic shapes supported on pre-stressed pillars of great slenderness. As the development of the pillar from Norman to Perpendicular was one of progressive fining down, the logical idea was to continue this process. But why have pillars at all? No doubt this was possible, but I was convinced that aisles with some physical division from the nave would help liturgical movement and that the occasional interval of a slender pillar would give dignity and a certain remoteness to a procession passing down the aisle. They would also give perspective to the interior and be a counterpoint to the stone slabs of the outer walls.

The choir stalls should, I thought, look like old ones on first glance. This is an English Cathedral and they should all have canopies. I designed a perforated canopy made out of laminated timber—mahogany and birch.

About the time the competition was announced, the Arts Council had held an exhibition of tapestries by famous British artists. The tapestries were all made by the Edinburgh Tapestry Company, owned by the Bute family. I had been struck by the brilliance of the colours and the non-reflective quality that tapestry has and I was particularly attracted to one of Wading Birds by Graham Sutherland. I have always admired his work and his painting of the Crucifixion at Northampton had made a deep impression on me. When I went to the old Coventry Cathedral for the first time I decided that a great tapestry, the height of the nave, should hang behind the altar, and that if I was successful in the competition, I would ask Graham Sutherland to design it and the Edinburgh Tapestry Company to weave it.

The materials of everything were chosen with care. This building was being designed for a life of at least 500 years and all pervious materials had to be avoided. The final choice for the exterior was stone, glass, copper (to cover the roof), hardwood, lead and bronze. On the competition drawings the interior was the same stone as the outside, a marble floor and concrete vault. Concrete was not allowed to come directly in contact with the English climate.

But the difficulties were great. It was a hard struggle. In the Middle Ages many cathedrals were building and one could, I imagine, discuss problems with many people concerned in the same enterprise, as an architect today can discuss the designs of, say, a school. But I found myself absolutely alone and there were few people I could talk to who understood or could help. The desert, however, has its attractions and I got to know the Brandenburg Concertos by heart, as I played them over and over again while I worked late into the night.

Two people encouraged and helped me during this lonely period: my wife who was the reinforcement in the concrete, and my friend Count 'Jas Tarnowski, a Polish refugee, widely travelled, very erudite and a ruthless critic.

The time drew near to handing in. All the drawings except the large-scale detail were complete, although the report was only partly written. It had been a deep spiritual experience and I had gained a great deal in the process of working out the design. If I now submitted it I would dilute or even destroy this feeling of deep contentment. I should not turn it to practical account. I should not hand in. Then I asked my wife for her opinion.

'You have sweated all these months,' she said. 'You hand in and don't be such an ass.'

I completed the detail drawing and report and delivered the drawings personally to Captain Thurston, Secretary of the Reconstruction Committee, on the last day. There were many other architects doing the same thing.

CHAPTER 4

The Result

THERE IS ALWAYS a feeling of anti-climax after handing in which gradually disappears as the date the results are due gets nearer. I know the feeling well, for I have been in for many competitions, although none approaching this one in importance.

I can say with truth I did not have the faintest hope of success. I felt certain that some bright young boy would come along and win it. I felt, however, that as a pace-maker my plan was not bad, and right up to the 15th August 1951, when the results would be announced, I was interested but expected nothing.

But whatever the chances, the period of waiting is one of post mortems—the design was with me constantly, day and night.

I did not know how my quiet drawings would strike the judges. My drawings were all in pencil, lightly tinted in a pale grey; the drawings had a silvery quality, but they didn't shout. The Conditions debarred shadows, which was a pity as I had designed a building which would cast strong shadows. I knew that when the judges examined my set they would realise this; but shadows would have given weight and scale.

Inevitably I went over the plan with a magnifying glass. I was greatly concerned about the Chapel of Unity, as it was made clear in the Conditions that a view of the altar from this Chapel would be an advantage. I felt strongly that the altar—the Anglican altar—should not be seen from here but I did not feel this about the font. The Sacrament of Baptism is accepted by all Christian denominations;

17

but an altar vested with Cross, candlesticks and ornaments would not be so welcome. Even in the Church of England there is much discussion as to how the Holy Table should be vested.

In my report I had developed the idea of the stained glass. Architecturally I did not want a flat light all through the nave. In Ravenna I had seen the beautiful golden light that penetrated the alabaster windows, and I wanted this quality of light round the altar. In order to appreciate this there would have to be a strong contrast nearby.

I started with the huge baptistry window, which is larger than the east window at Gloucester, and planned here a series of lights in bright primary colours. (It should be remembered that as one enters the Cathedral the only window that will be seen will be the one behind the font. All others will shine towards the altar.) I knew I was right to do this as I wanted the Holy Table to be dominant, backed by the great tapestry. So, progressing towards the altar, the five pairs of windows reveal themselves as you reach them. My idea was to represent in colour the stages from birth to afterlife, and the first pair of windows represent youth; these would be predominantly green—the young shoots.

Then the age of passion—the next pair—carried out in predominantly red colours. Middle life, with all the patchwork of experience—joys and sorrows, triumphs and disasters, were planned as a kaleidoscope of colours, bright and sombre, light and dark.

From these to old age and the richness of experience and wisdom. This pair in deep purple, dark blue flecked with patches of silver and gold; sombre and dignified, they would make a fitting prelude to the altar windows which I wanted mainly in golden glass. There should be a burst of golden light round the altar. In my mind's eye it seemed all right but it was hard to be sure as I had not seen this arrangement in any church.

If the altar is to be seen, appreciated, and be an invitation to

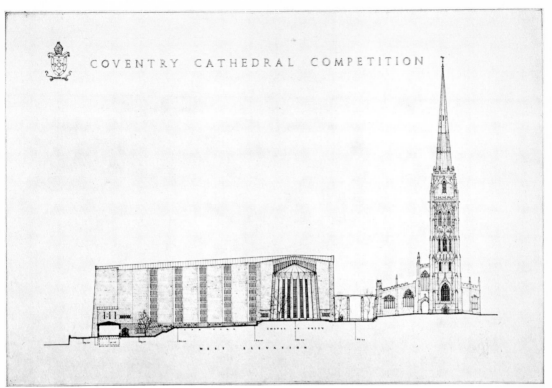

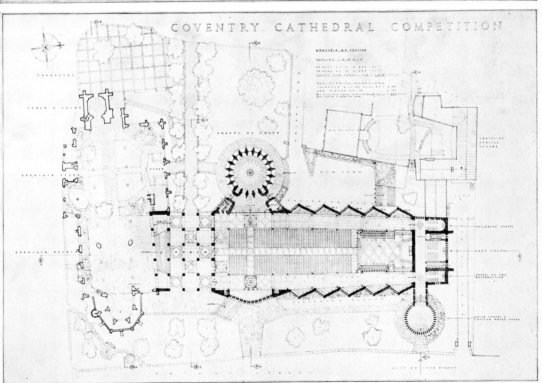

4 and 5. *Two of the set of competition drawings Basil Spence submitted in 1951. The original porch linking the ruins to the new building was far less prominent and the main approach was on the axis of the Baptistry window. The first Chapel of Unity design appears on the elevation.*

Communion, a bright window behind is, to my mind, a mistake. I have seen churches like this and in some cases it has been difficult even to see the altar.

I was also worried about the acoustics, as I know that in old churches the carved and moulded work on which dust settles provides a most effective acoustic absorbent, whereas hard, smooth surfaces give an undesirable echo. My design was very plain and completely devoid of mouldings—the only absorbent was the tapestry. I had not thought it worth while to get advice before I handed in, but now my doubts and fears gradually made themselves felt.

Came the 15th August; I had an appointment in London at 11.30 with the Secretary of Associated Electrical Industries, George Walker.

Business meetings with people I have never met are always a bit of a strain, however charming they may be, and I was rather on edge. In the middle of our discussion the telephone rang. George Walker answered it and said 'It's for you, they say it's important.'

I have always made it a rule that my office never telephone when I am with a client unless it is desperately important. Of course, my mind leapt to the Coventry result, and my first thought was that I had been awarded a place; second or third—but not first.

My secretary's voice said, 'Mr. Spence, good news! Here's Mr. Wearden,' and then Wearden, my Chief Assistant in London, said:

'May I be the first to congratulate you, you've won the competition.'

It is difficult to describe the next few moments, as I cannot remember them very well; swirling mists, a rushing sound in my ears, and I found myself on one of George Walker's comfortable chairs. He was bending over me, his expression all sympathy.

'I'm so terribly sorry, it must be awful news. You look ghastly,' he said.

I stammered, 'It's the best news I have ever had. I have won the Competition for the New Coventry Cathedral.'

Drinks were called for (I could have done with some strong whisky but perhaps George Walker was thinking 'Cathedral', for all I got was dry sherry). It was but the first of many such drinks, as I found that Anglican clergy favour it above all others.

Presently I left them. It was lunchtime but I felt I had to go to Saint Paul's Cathedral for a while. I went in and stayed under Christopher Wren's great dome quietly for about an hour. I felt a period of dedication was called for as I had a desperate need to be alone and to meditate quietly.

When I got back to the office they were in a complete flap. Everybody had been ringing up, practically every paper wanted an interview. I telephoned Edinburgh and spoke to my wife, asking my secretary to arrange my very first press conference for the afternoon, then went to the pub next door and had some roast beef sandwiches and coffee. The emotion that possessed me was one of great elation, that my life's wish had been granted; but with it came a strange humility, the awful feeling that the finger had pointed at me, and that I was not worthy or able.

I had the press conference, which was a bit of a shambles, in our small office in Buckingham Street, and then I took the whole office out to Gordon's Sherry Bar at the Watergate, but we all drank champagne. I can hardly remember the night train back to Edinburgh.

CHAPTER 5

The Awakening

FROM NOW ON the pace quickened. I realised that the old life had gone and that the glare of publicity was turned on me. This came as a shock and a surprise, although I had, of course, had an indication during the press conference in London.

The Competition Judges' report was most generous and left nothing in doubt: it was clear they were united and liked my design. (See Appendix D, page 131.) My thought of emigration to America melted like a snowflake in the sun; for my prayer had been granted, the tide had turned and now, I thought, all was ready for a period of great activity; now I should get all the 'solid' work I wanted.

Little did I realise I was not to receive a single commission, large or small, for two-and-a-half years, that I was to go almost bankrupt, that a bitter controversy was to rage over the design for the New Cathedral, that no licence to build would be forthcoming until a fortnight before building licences were abolished altogether.

When I arrived back in Edinburgh I was treading on air. There were excited discussions with my wife and my two partners in Scotland, Hardie Glover and Peter Ferguson. (Andrew Renton, my London partner, was away and had sent me a telegram.)

I saw the newspapers. Nearly all carried an illustration of the West Elevation, a technical drawing intended for the eye of the judges who could understand it, and not for a small reproduction in a newspaper. Most comments were complimentary but great stress

21

was laid on this 'revolutionary' design—the word 'concrete' was used often, stone hardly ever.

This came as a shock, for I thought it obvious that mine was a quiet design in the English tradition—the true tradition. And why did the papers emphasise the 'sensational'? Despite the many cheering telegrams I received from friends, I had a sinking feeling in my stomach.

We were invited to go down to Coventry immediately to attend a Civic Reception, and stayed the night *en route* at Fosse Bridge with our friends David and Tamara Talbot Rice. At a party that evening I was attacked by an Archdeacon who accused me of being revolutionary. Of course I defended my position with vigour and accused the Church of living in the past and betraying its heritage of being *the* patron of forward-looking architects. 'Where was the vitality?' I asked; but I got no satisfactory answer. As with the newspaper comments, I was surprised and pained by this attack but it was to be repeated many times by honest, sincere people who just did not understand my concepts.

At Coventry next morning, we went straight to the Henry the Eighth School where the 219 Competition designs were exhibited. They were hung everywhere, in corridors, classrooms and in the Great Hall. My set (number 91) was in the place of honour at the entrance to the Great Hall.

Captain Thurston, a cheerful, energetic person, introduced me. First to the Provost, whom I liked at once, then to the Chairman of the Reconstruction Committee, Mr. E. H. Ford, a gentle, nice man, and then to the Bishop, Neville Gorton. As I shook his hand I thought, 'Here is a real Bishop', for he had one of the most saintly of faces I have ever seen—which mirrored his character absolutely.

Then followed an excited discussion round the plans. The press wanted photographs, I was taken to meet the Mayor, I was introduced to Colonel Siddley, a member of the Committee, and I managed to get a quiet moment with the Provost. He said he believed that I had been inspired, but I could rely on him through thick and thin and that his life's ambition was to see Coventry's Cathedral rise again. I liked him more and more. Then the B.B.C. wanted an interview and at last we were whisked off to Saint Mary's Hall for the reception and lunch.

I found that I was placed far away from Joan, my wife, round the end of the top table. The top table was occupied by the chairman of this and that committee, and from their speeches it appeared to me that they had won the competition and not I. Still, it was their town and they were giving us lunch. Without being forewarned, I was asked to make a speech. I began to feel wary of the Coventry City Council.

However, the lunch was saved for me by a most encouraging talk to the three Competition Judges. I had met Sir Percy Thomas and Sir Howard Robertson before but never Sir Edward Maufe, whose charm, gentleness and sincerity now struck me forcibly. I already knew I had staunch allies in the Assessors. Sir Edward was to play an important part later in the struggle with the Royal Fine Arts Commission.

Back at the Exhibition, I was keen to look at the other designs, but this was difficult as I was a sort of curiosity to be shown to all and sundry; so I was always being pulled away to meet someone or other.

Two unsuccessful designs, however, made a strong impression on me. One was by Rolf Hellberg, who was disqualified because he had broken one of the Conditions: his plan did not allow liturgical movement. It was sad that all those months of work should be lost by disqualification, but the competition system, if it is to be maintained, must be governed rigidly and fairly.

The second design that impressed me was one submitted by Peter and Alison Smithson; a vast swooping concrete canopy, ingeniously supported, enclosed in a rectangle of glass wall. It was a simple, strong and electrifying design which strode over the old Cathedral and enclosed parts of the ruins, carried out with verve and conviction. But apart from the practical difficulties of the destruction of the old Cathedral and the maintenance of a huge clear glass area, I do not think it would ever have been built for it was certainly much more radical than the one I submitted, and my design had only just scraped through.

Some of the others were fantastic. One was a huge Cross many hundreds of feet high with a cathedral at the base; another (from Jamaica) appeared to be made up like a bowl of bananas and pineapples. One was entirely underground, as the designer thought that in view of the atom bomb the Cathedral should be a vast shelter. What a reflection on our times that an architect should seriously do this and spend hours preparing drawings!

Of course there was the expected crop of pure Gothic Revival buildings. Perhaps the most scholarly of these was that submitted by Sir Albert Richardson. His building occupied the entire site of the old Cathedral and therefore entailed pulling nine-tenths of it down and substituting his own brand of Gothic. The tower and spire and south porch were, as far as I could see, the only two parts of the old building that were kept. Why is it, I often ask, that the young architect respects work of the past and would certainly think twice before sweeping it away; whilst the traditional architect sometimes fails to respect it? As an example of this, witness the destruction by a Victorian of a Romanesque part of Saint Alban's Cathedral, replacing it with his own kind of early English.

Just before we went back to Edinburgh I had a quarter of an hour alone with the Provost. By now he knew my design backwards. My subject for the great tapestry had been the Crucifixion surmounted by the Risen Christ surrounded by the four beasts—Resurrection through the Passion. I had also taken the charred cross into the Cathedral to preserve it as a relic. The Provost suggested it would be more logical and in line with my primary idea to leave the Charred Cross in the apse, and to make the subject of the great tapestry 'Christ in Majesty'. He was, of course, quite right and from that moment the subject has been unchanged.

I returned to Edinburgh cheered by the support of those whose opinion I valued, but also filled with uncertainty and foreboding, for I saw now that the job of building the Cathedral was going to be a most difficult and testing task, not only because of its practical problems but also because of those involving publicity and personalities.

When we arrived home I got another shock. There were hundreds of letters, a few from friends but nearly all from strangers and these, if not abusive or downright insulting, were just plain critical. The majority were anonymous.

What warped minds the writers of anonymous letters must have, to take pen or pencil, or in one case lipstick (a proposal of marriage couched in obscene terms), and spend quite some time thinking up the rudest and most insulting phrases imaginable.

One epistle of three foolscap pages closely, legibly and neatly written, contained obscenities with a queer warped religious tinge to them. Some did not even have stamps, which shocked me as a Scot.

Some, though rude, had their twist of humour. One character, who did sign his letter and stamp it, wrote a critical and insulting two pages ending with 'yours malevolently', adding a postscript: 'If this gives you as much pleasure to tear up as it has given me to write, we will call it quits.'

These letters (which continued to come in for a long time) upset me so much that my wife used to read and destroy them before they got to me. But this usually sent *her* into a rage—I don't know which I would have preferred, the letters or the rage.

Months before the competition results were known we had arranged to spend a month on the Costa Brava in Spain. Our route, as usual, included cathedral towns and we had planned to stop at Albi. This visit was now of vital importance, but there was so much to be done before we could leave by car at the beginning of the last week in August.

One of the tasks was an urgent request for a perspective drawing for publication. I was so occupied I could not do this myself, so I asked a very talented architect, Laurence Wright, to do it for me. He came up to Edinburgh, stayed two days and worked the whole of one night to complete it. I shall always be grateful to him for this burst of activity, but we should have spent more time selecting the point of view as the one I asked him to do was not the best. Its reproduction seemed to make matters worse, for by now there was a full-blown controversy in quite a few of the newspapers, and by the time we were ready to leave for Spain the correspondence columns of the dailies carried several letters each day about the design, most of which were adversely critical.

I was glad when we were bowling along the roads of France heading south to Spain (although even there, somewhere near Rocamadour, an Englishman came up to me and said 'Are you Basil Spence, architect for that modern concrete cathedral at Coventry') and my tension began to ease.

What an impact the great brick church of Albi has as it dominates the tile-covered houses that nestle close to it, like a great brown hen with hundreds of chicks. The fortress-like walls rise with uncompromising sheerness to the full height. One cannot see

26

6. *Albi Cathedral. The Porch. A sketch by Basil Spence.*

the roof, but the tower, strong with part-cylinder buttresses, is majestic.

The rhythm of the outer walls is interesting and original, as the buttresses are half-round on plan and not rectangular as in our cathedrals. In between the buttresses are tall lancelot-like windows of very simple tracery. The bricks are a beautiful warm pink. Below the parapet is a decorated corbel which is the only piece of enrichment on this vast mass of brick and tall vertical punctuation of narrow windows and buttresses. There is no cathedral in England so simple and at the same time so dramatic.

The interior is extremely rich but it lacks space as, like Burgos, it is interrupted by the choir. Nevertheless this building is a masterpiece, poised, dignified, with a breathtaking simplicity. If only Coventry could have some of that quality. The South Porch, preceded by some magnificently designed steps, is very elaborate—as elaborate, I thought, as the old Cathedral at Coventry; and the cathedral itself is just as plain as mine. I was deeply stirred and stimulated.

Our hotel on the Costa Brava could not have been better situated, as it was pitched on some rocks overlooking the Mediterranean, with a private beach. Though not what one could call a brilliant architectural composition, it nevertheless hugged the rocks, and the terraces and approaches were well laid out.

Here was the place to relax and rest. But a well-known voice said, 'Are you Basil Spence?' It was John Arlott. I could not escape my task—perhaps I did not really want to, so the next day I started on some perspective interiors of the cathedral. (John turned out to be a staunch supporter of the design. He understood it well and after we returned to London he wrote a strongly *pro* article for his paper—a welcome piece of encouragement in the high tide of criticism.)

I did four interiors and one exterior, all in oil paints. I had in any case intended to indulge my hobby of dabbling away in oils, as I love to abstract a landscape. I was glad to have this time to think and go over my design.

Two buildings near us made an important contribution to the development of the design, one in Barcelona and the other in Gerona.

About half a century ago an architectural genius worked in Barcelona. His name was Antonio Gaudi. Occasionally history throws up an individual who thinks for himself, has strong convictions and works in spite of everybody. Such a man was Gaudi. He conceived a great stone church in the middle of Barcelona, a most original organic design of enormous size, scale and imagination. Work was started about the same time as on the Anglican cathedral in Liverpool, but only a fragment of his design was built. It stands proudly, a challenge and a symbol.

Only the west front with the four banana-like towers gives any idea of the scope and magnificence of the final design. Though much of the sculptured carving was bad to my eye and some of the forms were strange to me, I was excited beyond measure. Here was stone used in a plastic, organic way and completely without inhibitions. Surmounting the four towers are imaginative, fantastic finials of coloured and gold mosaic of enormous size; they might have been done by Picasso. Each tower has a stair winding upward. Each is a piece of sculpture in its own right. The buttresses, pinnacles and arches make, for me, a most wonderful composition.

Now, in the 1960's Gaudi is having a strong influence on the current thought of students working in our schools of architecture. The young architect is turning away from the glass box to the greener, lusher pastures of plastic expression. Perhaps the most successful exponent is the architect Le Corbusier, whose work in India, the Convent of La Tourette and the beautiful Chapel at Ronchamp are all good examples of plastic architecture at its best.

Gerona, a few miles from our hotel, also has a beautiful cathedral.

The Awakening

It possesses a nave with one of the widest spans in the world. However, it was not this feat of engineering that attracted me, but the approach to the west front preceded by a flight of one hundred wide steps. The sweep and dramatic effect is magnificent and there is something poetic in the picture made by small figures toiling up to this shrine. These steps are even better, to my mind, than those wide processional approaches at Versailles.

For some time I had been critical of the porch in my competition design. Now I began to think it mean and puny, not a strong enough link between the new and the old. I was worried, too, about the great glass screen which I had planned to lower so as to throw the Cathedral open. Was this really good? Was it not only a gimmick? Coventry is not the cleanest of places. Dead leaves, dust and cigarette packets would blow into the Cathedral. Was it worth it?

Walking up the steps at Gerona I decided to raise the porch to the full height of the vault, to make it a fixed glass screen of enormous size and carry the glass engraving over the whole surface. I would approach this great porch by a flight of steps and on the right would be the figure of Saint Michael—for Coventry is the cathedral church of Saint Michael.

From a practical point of view, this porch would also help the Cathedral, for my competition porch had side steps, an arrangement not very convenient for weddings or even funerals. My new idea was much better.

I had been told that the Reconstruction Committee were unanimous in accepting my design and that the Cathedral Council were unanimous with only one abstention. Now I would have to go back and tell them that I wished to alter the design in these particulars. I must put on record that although the ten years have been full of these amendments and, I hope, improvements, never once has the Reconstruction Committee itself asked me to amend even the smallest detail. I have always gone to them with suggestions and their approval has always been given generously and with encouragement.

CHAPTER 6

Down to Earth

ON OUR RETURN from holiday two main tasks confronted me: the presentation of the plans to the Royal Fine Art Commission and the drawings for the model which was to be submitted for the Summer Exhibition of the Royal Academy. This meant complete $\frac{1}{8}$ scale plans not only of the exterior and amended porch, but also of the interior.

I had a feeling that I would have a rough time with the Royal Fine Art Commission. I knew that there was some strong opposition to my design. On the other hand I also knew that two members, Sir Edward Maufe and Sir Howard Robertson, were staunch supporters, as well as Sir William Holford and Sir John Summerson.

One day in late autumn I was summoned to attend and explain the scheme and answer questions at a meeting of the Technical Committee of the Royal Fine Art Commission. I have been a member of the Commission for several years now and I am always sympathetic to architects who come to see us, as I know what an ordeal it can be.

I must say I was received kindly enough. Sir Edward Maufe was friendly and helpful and so were Holford and Summerson. Another member, Sir Albert Richardson, stood looking out of the window and did not say a word. I said what I had to say and thought the occasion had gone off well enough; but when the next day I tried to find out the results of the meeting (naturally enough, as Sir Giles Gilbert Scott's design had been wrecked on this rock) Godfrey

Samuel, the secretary, told me that a decision had been postponed. He was very official in his manner and gave me no comfort.

Meanwhile, the *Architectural Review* of January 1952 carried an article written by its editor, J. M. Richards. I have always admired Jim Richards for his honesty and sincerity, but it was painfully obvious by the tone of his essay that he was completely out of sympathy with my design and if the drawings conveyed any of my feelings to him he must have discounted them as worthless. Moreover, this came at a time when I was at my lowest ebb of confidence and it made me even more depressed. The article did me great harm abroad, and when I went to Canada with the Provost in 1953 to appeal for funds, many people referred to it, even quoting actual passages from it: criticisms that were by then woefully out of date.

However, there was one break in the clouds; Professor Nikolaus Pevsner, one of the Board of Editors of the *Architectural Review*, came out on my side with a B.B.C. talk on the Third Programme. This talk was published in *The Listener* and did much to counter the unfavourable criticisms in the architectural press as a whole. (Here I must acknowledge the staunch support given to me ever since the design was published by Ian Leslie, Editor of *The Builder*.)

It was in this atmosphere of criticism and doubt that the Royal Fine Art Commission made its final decision. It approved the design in guarded terms, adding nonetheless that my design 'was capable of resulting in a fine building'. I know now there were bitter arguments and agreement was hard to reach, that Sir Edward and Sir Howard had to work hard.

Sir Albert Richardson, however, was far from satisfied at the way things were going. He was a member of the Central Council for the Care of Churches, a body composed of distinguished clergymen, peers and others high in their respective professions. It had been asked to examine and comment on my design. The object of this Council was certainly a noble one; but I failed to see why I should be put on the carpet, when I was preserving intact the entire remnants of the existing Coventry Cathedral.

I had refused to send my plans in beforehand as I am a great believer in explaining a plan at first hand. Misconceptions often arise when no explanation is available and once a view has been expressed it is sometimes difficult for important people to climb down.

Lord Mottestone, the architect, and his partner Paul Paget took me to lunch beforehand at the House of Lords (to give me courage), for the Council meets in the Jerusalem Chamber of Westminster Abbey close by. My assistant arrived with the drawings at the appointed time and I took them in myself. The magnificent room hung with tapestries was full of important clergymen and peers, with several architects. Sir Albert himself was absent.

The Chairman invited me to explain my design. I was standing next to the Dean of Windsor, Bishop Hamilton, and I shall always be grateful for his grunts of encouragement. First of all I pointed out that they need have no qualms about the care of the old fabric of Coventry Cathedral; I had already given instructions for its repair and maintenance against further damage from the elements. Then I explained my views about tradition, that I was trying to be traditional, that here in Westminster Abbey we could witness tradition at first hand and that I envied the courage of the architect of Henry the Seventh's Chapel who could make his walls so zig-zag. 'If only I had that courage,' I said.

I explained the idea of the design. I told them of the materials (there was surprise when I mentioned it was built of stone); I spoke of the tapestry, which was to be the largest in the world, representing Christ in Majesty; I said that the new building would stand for the triumph of the Resurrection with the old representing the Sacrifice.

I spoke for two hours.

When I had done there was a silence. Then came a few questions and then I was told their decision should be taken in private. I retired, feeling as if I had been chewed and spat out again.

Next day I heard the decision: it was that I should be encouraged to develop my design unmolested.

7. *The flight of stone steps leading to the Porch into the entrance through the Great West Screen to the right; the ruins to the left and beyond the Porch is the Holy Trinity Church. The walls and columns are in a pinky-grey local sandstone.*

CHAPTER 7

The Beginning of the Long Haul

LATE in 1951, I presented the model drawings to the Reconstruction Committee for their approval. They included the revised porch and all were approved with enthusiasm. Work was started on the model.

It is seldom realised how expensive these constructions are. We got several quotations from reputable model-makers and all were between three and four thousand pounds—the price of quite a nice house pre-war. But Fred Keil, of the City Display Organisation, who had carried out many designs during my exhibition days, asked if he could help. I told him that the Reconstruction Committee had put aside one thousand pounds for the purpose. He replied, 'If that is all you have got I suppose that is all I will get', and he produced one of the most beautiful models I have ever seen. The interior lit up, everything was there, even the choir stalls, grilles and the font cover. I know it cost him many times the amount he got for it.

This model was shown in the Royal Academy Summer Exhibition of 1952 and several critics cited it as the 'Picture of the Year', an honour seldom, if ever, handed out to an architectural work in the Royal Academy.

About this time Edward Maufe asked me if I would agree to my name going forward as a candidate for the Royal Academy.

Work now began to get into its practical stride and technical and administrative matters crowded on all sides.

At one of the early meetings of the Reconstruction Committee I had asked them to appoint the engineer for the structure, and the artist to design the great tapestry. To my mind the best engineer to understand the aesthetic point of view, and a brilliant professional, was Ove Arup; and of course I wanted Graham Sutherland for the great tapestry.

The Committee agreed to my recommendations and I was asked to approach the two men. Ove Arup accepted with pleasure but Graham Sutherland was more guarded and said he would like to think about it. He was staying in a studio flat at Villefranche-sur-Mer in the south of France and suggested I should fly out and discuss the matter. It was January, I had a threatened slipped disc—a disc on the move, shall we say—so I went to Villefranche-sur-Mer with alacrity.

Graham and Kathy Sutherland met me at Nice Airport. It was lovely and warm and I felt better immediately.

I had brought a set of plans and photographs of my perspective drawings, as Graham had seen only press illustrations, and we had a thorough discussion of the design.

He followed my descriptions attentively, putting a question here and there. He was sensitive and charming: I liked him and Mrs. Sutherland at once; and I was certain he would make a masterpiece of this great tapestry which, as the world's largest, was a unique opportunity for any artist.

I think Graham hesitated at the beginning because he wanted to reflect on the magnitude of the task, to find out if he could work with me and what conditions were entailed. He is an artist with an international reputation which could be seriously impaired if things were to go wrong on a project of this size, with the glare of publicity on it. So, looking over the little harbour of Villefranche with the small boats gently heaving in the brilliant sunshine, we went on with our discussions. At that time I had the tapestry planned immediately behind the altar, with a wall dividing the nave from the lady chapel, which was on the other side to the north. The tapestry, of course, rose to the full height of about 70 feet and it was about 44 feet across —a vast area.

Graham thought the proportions a trifle squat: he said he preferred an upright proportion, and I pigeon-holed this observation for the future. I told him I wanted, almost as an architectural necessity, a figure of Christ 30 feet to 35 feet high, a great majestic figure surrounded by the four beasts and bringing in, if possible, the Apostles. He welcomed conditions of this kind, he said, as then he knew where he stood and he liked the first painting of the interior that I had done in Spain as it had 'the feeling of tapestry', as he put it. It is remarkable how closely the final design resembles the general lines of my first sketch.

We then read the relevant passages of the Book of Revelation:

And immediately I was in the spirit: and, behold a throne was set in heaven, and one sat on the throne.

And he that sat was to look upon like a jasper and a sardine stone; and there was a rainbow round about the throne in sight like unto an emerald.

And in the midst of the throne, and round about the throne were four beasts ... and the first beast was like a lion, and the second beast like a calf, and the third beast has a face as a man, and the fourth beast was like a flying eagle.

which is Chapter IV, verses 2, 3, 6 and 7. And also Chapter XII, verses 7, 8 and 9:

And there was a war in heaven: Michael and his angels fought against the dragon; and the dragon fought and his angels, and prevailed not, neither was their place found any more in heaven. And the great dragon was cast out, that old serpent called the Devil, and Satan, which deceiveth the whole world, he was cast out into the earth, and his angels were cast out with him.

I observed that in the traditional representation of the Beasts they are often shown without the many characteristics described in the

Scripture—'Full of eyes, before and behind', 'six wings', for example.
I still feel that the representation of the Beasts in the final design is the
most imaginative in the history of this subject.

We talked about colour and I had a glimpse into the mind of a
great colourist: the strangeness of his choice, green and mauve, black,
orange, brassy yellow, magneta. But the main background had to
be muted because of the pinky-grey stone of the interior. Graham
told me that this colour was a great restriction to the artist.

In fact we ranged over the whole problem. The design, and how
to implement it. Right from the beginning I was convinced that the
cartoon should be done small—not higher than 7 feet—and photographed up to full size. This would retain the vitality of the smaller
design. We agreed about this; indeed we found agreement on all
questions.

I stayed with the Sutherlands for a week. Of course we did not
work all the time but drove about the countryside and two of the
places we visited made a strong impression on me. The first was
Matisse's Chapel at Vence and the other Picasso's exhibition of
painting and pottery at the Musée d'Antibes.

Vence lies near Nice and inland just before the ground rises up
to the Alpes Maritimes. It is not the hill town of St. Paul-en-Vence,
and Matisse's Chapel is placed in rather a banal position in a typical
French street of bourgeois character.

Architecturally the exterior is almost vulgar, roofed as it is in
ghastly, highly glazed, ultramarine half-round tiles; but it is surmounted by a wrought iron belfry of interesting and idiosyncratic
design which, with the beautiful tile tympanum over the entrance
doorway, show the calibre of the master.

The inside is entirely different from the outside—like Ravenna,
sotto voce outside, *forte* inside. The walls, ceiling and floor are vast
areas of white, with a little black marble set into the white marble

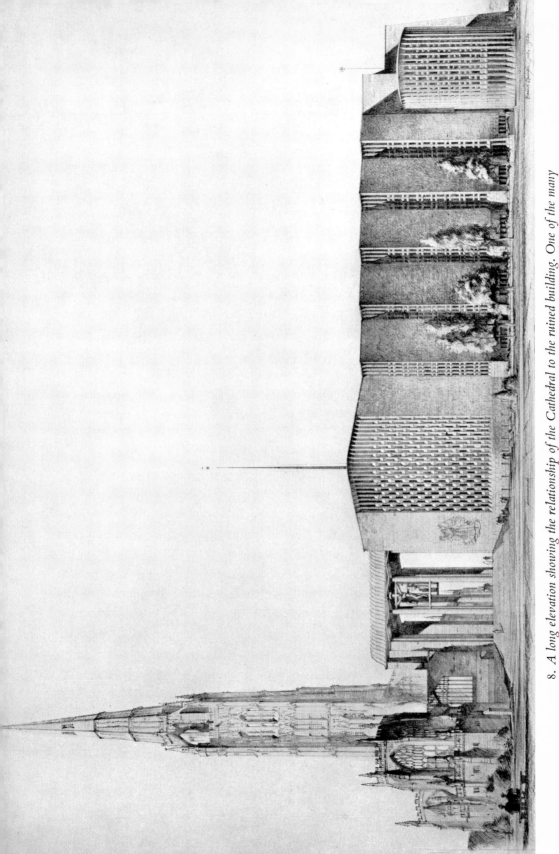

8. A long elevation showing the relationship of the Cathedral to the ruined building. One of the many drawings carried out over the years to illustrate developments in the design. July 1952.

9. *An early scale model. The ruined apse, the porch and the Baptistry window.*

10. *The interior. The rearrangement of the Chancel to bring the High Altar forward by setting the clergy stalls and choir around it. Although this grouping was not adopted, the drawing shows Basil Spence's conception of a huge tapestry of Christ hung on the wall behind the altar even before Sutherland was approached to prepare a design for it. November 1951.*

11. *The aisle, with the walls, the Tablets of the Word, the bench seats and one half of the organ reflected in the polished black marble floor. Beyond and beneath the organ can be seen the Gethsemane Chapel.*

floor. The altar, however, is a honey-coloured travertine of a strong, plain design, set at an angle in the simple rectangular chapel. Some stalls of indifferent design are in natural timber.

But what bowled me over was the quality of light that played on those white surfaces. It was like walking into a pearl. Matisse's stained-glass windows are basically bright blue, purple and gold in very thin glass, to admit a great deal of coloured light. His famous decorations have a deceptive simplicity and are painted in a black line on white tile, all highly glazed. The effect of these white glazed surfaces in rectangular patches on the walls is highly successful, as the colours from the windows give a shimmering over-lay of blue and gold as one moves slowly round.

His figure of Saint Dominic behind the altar is utterly simple, a distillation of thought and work. In dignity it reminded me of the saints in St. Appollinare Nuovo in Ravenna, yet it was absolutely of our own time, to my mind a masterpiece of simplification and the search for truth. I do not think his other panels are quite so successful.

The door to the confessional is enchanting. A piece of carved wooden pierced work, faithfully following Matisse's own drawing, it is painted white; behind and glowing through the small openings is pure purple light. The effect of this discord is truly magical.

The actual architecture, generally speaking, is commonplace. One could almost call it bathroom architecture, as even the ceiling lights are simple glass spheres such as one sees in bathrooms. But the quality of light on the white makes it a unique place for me and it has the fundamental feeling of a chapel, a place of worship.

The Mediterranean practically laps the walls of the Musée d'Antibes, a small fortified castle of simple character which provides an excellent background for Picasso's work. The interior walls are finished in pure white plaster of a fairly rough texture, and the ceilings are of natural timber with beams and joists showing. Picasso's pictures and ceramics look superb against this simple setting with glimpses of the blue Mediterranean through the windows. Amongst this display were several tapestries of remarkable quality, woven in Aubusson, one designed by Roualt, another by Dufy, several by Picasso. It was clear that the French knew how to weave tapestry and the interpretation was superb. Graham was most interested and asked me if the Edinburgh Tapestry Company could do as well. I felt that for the large one we had in mind they should be just as good, if he controlled the weavers.

Before I left, Graham said he would let me know definitely very soon if he could accept the commission. I said good-bye to them and my optimism was only temporarily allayed by one of the roughest flights across the Alps I have ever experienced.

CHAPTER 8

The Central Altar, the Music and Acoustics

DR. NEVILLE GORTON, the late Bishop of Coventry, was
a saint. I have never met such a 'good' man, and one who had no
sense of possessiveness whatsoever; he desired nothing except the
things of the spirit. When the Archbishop of Canterbury said at his
funeral 'He was surrounded by gusts of the Holy Spirit', he was
right.

He was also a great character and dressed in the most bizarre
fashion. One got used to seeing him walking the streets of Coventry
with a serene far-away expression, wearing a dilapidated overcoat,
on his head a deerstalker with flies hooked into it, heavy woollen
stockings on his spindly legs, and if he didn't have on a huge under-
graduate's scarf, one caught a glimpse of purple under his clerical
collar. Sometimes he didn't even have a clerical collar but an
ordinary collar and tie.

Late in 1951 he invited me to dinner at the Liberal Club in
London to meet an old friend of his, Father C. E. Douglas. This
was the first of many meetings and I learnt more than I can say by
simply sitting quietly and listening to the discussion on Liturgy.
This was a fertile period for me; Neville Gorton fed me spiritually.

The Bishop was always champion of the central altar or a plan
that gave easy access to Holy Communion. He was against the
shut-in choir, the barrier that one finds in York and many other
cathedrals, the choir screen that shuts off the altar from the people.
In my Competition plan I had placed the altar at the end of the

41

main axis, as a climax. I had, however, been careful to place it so that it could be easily seen from all parts of the nave. I did not even show a communion rail as I thought this was an interruption and a visually disturbing element. My altar was placed in the traditional position beyond the choir and clergy stalls, but it was very open. Moreover it was raised, by a series of steps and ramps, six feet above the level of the nave so that it could be seen above the heads of the congregation. I arranged these steps and ramps most carefully so as to give the illusion that the altar was hardly raised above floor level, as I felt that the flight of steps so evident in some of the Renaissance churches gave an impression of aloofness and unavailability to the Holy Table.

The Bishop and Father Douglas discussed with me the possibility of bringing the altar right forward to the edge of the choir steps and putting the choir—and, indeed, the Clergy and the Bishop's throne —back behind the altar. (I illustrate one of my drawings of this arrangement.)

Both the Bishop and Douglas liked the idea of no communion rail. But what of old people who find it difficult to get upright without the help of a rail? And there is no doubt that the level shelf greatly facilitates the administering of Holy Communion by giving an even, horizontal position for all hands.

The Bishop, however, talked in a wonderful way about the gathering of the flock, saying that they should kneel anywhere on the three altar steps and that the Sacrament should be given individually to each. Perhaps we could have a short length of communion rail at the sides so that old people who wished to use it could do so—the weakest to the wall—rather like the old cathedrals where people knelt on the floor but stone seats were provided against the walls of the nave for those who were physically unable to kneel for long periods.

We discussed the function and position of the choir in the Church

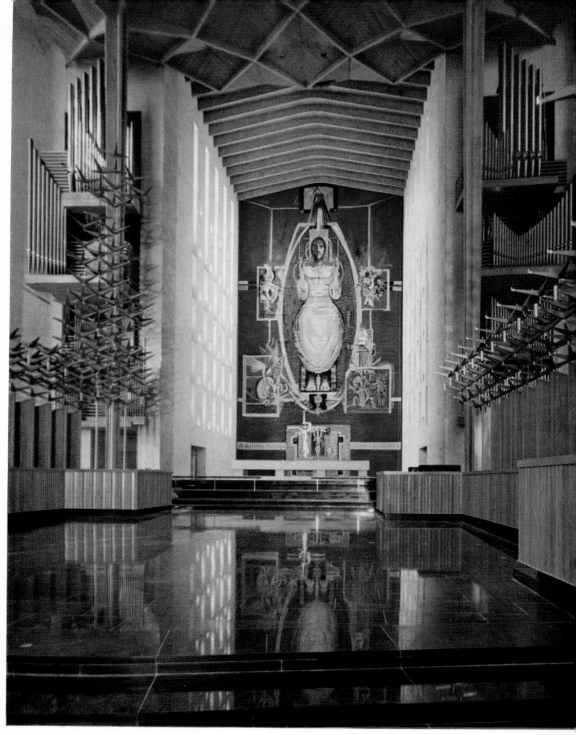

12. *The Nave, the High Altar framed by the Clergy Stalls and the Organ, backed by Graham Sutherland's tapestry.*

of England Liturgy. In the Reformed Church the service is a choral one with a great deal of singing in which the congregation is encouraged to take an important part, and the choir can be a great help in leading the singing. But the Bishop was impatient with this point of view, as he asserted that the Sacrament of Communion was the important thing and singing quite secondary; in any case, he said, the average choirboy was a scruffy, fidgeting individual who should be put out of sight. (I may say I have never seen a more fidgety person than the Bishop himself, especially when he was officiating. Although his services were wonderful experiences and Christian to the core, one never really knew what would happen next.)

We talked of the position of the canons and clergy, the Provost's stall and the Precentor; there were many problems to be solved in this arrangement. At Ravenna and in northern Italy I had seen several early Christian churches which came almost directly from the Court of Justice Basilica of Roman times; behind the high altar and on the main axes were the Clergy and the Bishop's throne was in the centre.

After discussion, this was the plan on which we finally decided. The altar was brought right forward with only three steps up from the nave, so that the Holy Table itself could be strong, big and simple. Immediately behind would be the choir and somehow an organ console would have to be fitted in; and beyond that the Clergy stalls in a 'U' shape, with the Bishop's throne in the centre on the axis.

Dr. Gorton fidgeted and said, 'I don't want to be in the centre.' But he liked the plan and was willing to back it in the Reconstruction Committee. Father Douglas, however, said it did not go far enough and he wanted a huge canopy over the altar suspended or supported on four pillars—a Baldechino. As there is no rule about this in our Rubric, I objected, as I felt it was an extra element to clutter up the space and it would be an obstruction to the vision of the great tapestry.

There were other architectural snags; for instance, I had wished to create a pool of golden light round the altar, the golden windows being the last pair. Now that the altar was being brought forward it would be in the mauve light. Perhaps a good thing, but I was far from certain. Why not change the golden windows then? But this would spoil the sequence of light down the nave. However I was willing to have the golden light behind if the plan for a new altar position was accepted.

Thus it went on. After each discussion I did a new plan which became the subject of a discussion which in turn produced yet another plan.

The plans were presented to the Reconstruction Committee and the Cathedral Council. They caused a near riot. On no account would either body accept this new arrangement of the High Altar; some members even threatened resignation. The Chairman of the Reconstruction Committee, Mr. Ford, was especially adamant about this and the whole idea was thrown out lock, stock and barrel. I was asked to revert to the original plan for the chancel.

In an Anglican cathedral the organ, choir and question of acoustics are all vitally important, and as the subject is specialised I asked the Reconstruction Committee if I might take advice from two consultants, one for the organ and choir and another for acoustics. The Chairman suggested we should appoint some famous organist and choirmaster and, as he had knowledge of organs and their specification and was an amateur organist himself, he suggested Sir Ernest Bullock, lately organist of Westminster Abbey and now Professor of Music in Glasgow University.

I was willing to take his advice in this respect and at the request of the Committee I got in touch with Sir Ernest. He appeared interested and agreed to act as our adviser on all musical matters, but when it came to the organ specification he asked that two other eminent organists should be drawn in as a small panel of advisers, suggesting Dr. Dykes Bower, St. Paul's Cathedral organist, and Dr. H. K. Andrews. The Committee of course approved.

So far as acoustics were concerned the only person I knew by reputation was Hope Bagnall, an architect who had lectured on the subject and was accepted as an authority. He had advised on the acoustics of the Royal Festival Hall. The Committee approved my choice and I wrote to him.

His reply came as a bit of a shock. He said he disagreed fundamentally with my design, that he contested the 'Shrine' idea, and supported the 'Auditorium', that the Cathedral would be useless if the spoken word was difficult to hear—I agreed with this, of course.

I got the impression that he disliked my design, but I was certain that if I met him I could explain my point of view and I wanted the chance to say I was quite willing to change the plan within reasonable limits. I wrote telling him this, suggested a meeting before he finally decided to refuse, and he came to my office.

He was a charming person, tall and spare with a serene expression, a gentle manner and one of the most beautiful speaking voices I have ever heard; but in his eye I detected the steely flint of the puritan.

In a long discussion of the plans he said he thought the volume of the nave was too great for really good acoustics, that the reverberation interval was 'too long'. I asked if amendments should be made to the surfaces (as the interior was stone and the vault concrete) but he said the absorption of these surfaces was practically nil and asked if I couldn't have tapestries hanging in each bay of the nave. He considered that the tapestry at the 'east' end was the only good thing acoustically about my design.

How was it, I asked, that cathedrals like Exeter and Durham were very good acoustically but had the same volume and indeed were

45

very near the height of my vault? I got the impression that he thought we should try and do better than these buildings, and in any case, these naves were heavily moulded so that dust, the friend of the acoustic expert, settled on all ledges and gave the desired surfaces for a good acoustic effect.

He left in a reasonably happy state of mind, I thought, and I sent him on a set of plans that evening.

Two days later I got an uncompromising letter from him. He opened it with a phrase to the effect that he had 'examined the plans with a heavy heart' and he went on to criticise my design from an architectural point of view, even externally, asking why I had not introduced string courses to throw off the weather? His last suggestion was that I should reduce the whole height by ten feet in the interests of 'anonymity'—which would have turned my design into a dumpy thing and not what I had been chosen to carry out. The internal proportions would be absolutely ruined. I wrote in answer saying that our collaboration would not be fruitful and he agreed.

I was now really worried and telephoned two architect friends for their advice. F. R. S. Yorke suggested William Allen of the Building Research Station. He had done a lot of the spade work on the Royal Festival Hall along with his colleague Stacy, and their reputation as acoustic experts was very high. Next I telephoned Robert Matthew, architect for the Royal Festival Hall. He confirmed Yorke's recommendation.

From now on acoustics, organ and choir were bound together and I had a preliminary meeting with Sir Ernest Bullock. He said that Messrs. Harrison and Harrison, the organ builders at Durham, were

(Opposite) *This group of the following seven interiors records the evolution of the design from the first model to the final one; from the first painting done in Spain in 1951 to the last perspective exhibited in the Royal Academy Summer Exhibition in 1958.*

13. *The interior seen through the engraved glass screen. Model.*

14. *The first painting done immediately after winning the competition in September 1951. The fundamentals are there: the plain cliffs of wall with panels of relief sculpture, the delicate canopy, the tapestry, the organ ranged up on each side.*

15. *The advent of the vault facetted like a fly's eye instead of smoothly rounded. The columns tapering down to a pinpoint connection with the floor. The quality of light streaking across the walls is foreseen. August 1952.*

16. *By February 1953 the wall on which the tapestry hangs behind the High Altar has been removed entirely and replaced by a reredos. The tapestry is now hung on the wall of the Lady Chapel, 50 feet farther back. In this way the volume of the Lady Chapel is added to that of the main body of the Cathedral.*

17. *The scale model made in 1953 which was exhibited at the Brussels exhibition in 1958. The facetted concrete canopy has been perforated. For the first time one of Graham Sutherland's designs for the tapestry has been included. The figure of Christ is portrayed with arms outstretched.*

18. *This perspective illustrates several major design developments: the introduction of a rough textured white plaster on the walls replacing the stone; the use of slatted spruce pyramids between concrete beams in the canopy; the final tapestry design; incised inscriptions and symbols on the wall panels instead of relief sculpture; the striped floor of marble. March 1958.*

19. *The interior of the final model as seen through the Great West Screen. The High Altar has become even more prominent and the reredos behind it has been removed entirely.*

20. *The Baptistry window and the Porch, beyond which can be seen the spire of the old Cathedral.*

21. *The deeply modelled stone Baptistry window, 81 feet high and 51 feet across, is glazed with stained glass designed by John Piper. It is a rich composition in colour culminating centrally in a clear blaze of golden light. Beneath it is the Font Boulder.*

22. *Looking down the full length of the Cathedral from the Porch steps past the Baptistry and Nave windows to the circular Chapel of Christ the Servant.*

23. *Inside the walls are covered in a rough textured white plaster which shows the brilliant sequence of colour of the nave windows to advantage. The thorn-like canopies of the clergy stalls appear in the foreground since this photograph was taken from within the Chancel.*

24. *Two bays of the nave showing the full height and proportions of the windows and cliff-like walls. An indication of the scale may be found in the stone bench seats at the base of the walls.*

25. *This huge screen of glass divides the porch from the nave. It has a bronze framework which is suspended from the roof on diagonal tension rods.*

26. *John Hutton putting the finishing touches to his engraved figures on the Great West Screen after they had been installed.*

the best for our purpose and he wanted their appointment so that the panel could work out a good specification with them. With some difficulty this was agreed by the Reconstruction Committee and the panel set to work.

But I wanted far more than a specification of an organ from Sir Ernest. I wanted his advice on the choir arrangements, also what acoustic properties we should aim at in the Cathedral. He said that two English cathedrals were almost perfect for the Anglican service, Durham and Exeter. He finally settled on Durham. This choice had the advantage that Harrisons had built the organ for Durham and, of course, knew the cathedral well.

'Bill' Allen and Stacy were told that they should match the acoustic qualities of Durham and all their deliberations, which have gone on through ten years of planning, have been directed to this object.

But what of the choir? When I showed my original plan to Sir Ernest he said it just would not do. The two sides of the choir were far too wide apart and they must be brought closer together. I had shown about twenty feet dividing the two sides, as this is about the distance in Liverpool Cathedral; but Sir Ernest said the choir would 'see-saw' and that ten feet was the maximum that could be accepted.

This, of course, worried me greatly as it would obscure the view of the altar. The choir would be a serious barrier and the character of the conception quite altered. I also knew what the Bishop thought about choirs and choirboys, and how he had accepted the altar in the back position if, and only if, it could be clearly seen and was not obstructed in any way.

I went to see the Provost and argued the whole matter with him. Of course, he took a balanced point of view and felt that there must be a compromise. He did not share the Bishop's views about choir boys, he liked to see them in front of the altar but he agreed that the altar must not be obstructed and suggested I should take Sir Ernest to see the Bishop.

Alas, as soon as I introduced them I knew it would be a stormy meeting.

The Bishop blasted away about choirs, the secondary importance of music in the church, the importance of Communion, the fundamental necessity of being able to see the altar clearly from the whole nave. I saw Ernest's face go redder and redder; I thought he would blow up. And he did. He presented his case with force and conviction, as an eminent musician and specialist.

I thought it was deadlock. How was it possible to reach agreement with two sides so far apart? But in the nick of time I got an idea; why not make the choir-stalls of separate movable units, like prayer desks, so that they could be moved at will according to the character of the service, and even removed altogether on occasions? In an instant I thought of another advantage: suppose they wished to do *The Messiah* with a vast choir? My arrangements allowed for expansion, and even if an orchestral concert were planned, this arrangement would cope with that too.

And so it was agreed. The quarrel was soon patched up and the Bishop and Sir Ernest parted friends.

CHAPTER 9

The Nave Glass

GRAHAM SUTHERLAND was appointed designer of the great tapestry early in the history of the new Cathedral because I foresaw delays and difficulties in the weaving. For the same reason I felt one or two other appointments should be made without delay: the engraver of the great glass screen and the stained glass artists for the windows in the nave.

I had no hesitation in recommending John Hutton for the great glass screen as he had worked with me on many exhibitions and I had found him an artist of great quality, a true draughtsman and one who knew the glass engraving technique backwards. Moreover he was a delight to work with, practical and trustworthy. The Committee appointed him immediately.

Provost Howard and John got together to work out the individual saints to be represented on this screen, and it was suggested that it should go up in layers of saints and angels so as to give scale. This idea was accepted and interpreted with great skill so that the effect now is of celestial 'cream cake' layers of saints and angels.

The first row consists of the five most famous Old Testament saints; the second, nine famous New Testament saints and the fourth and fifth consist of British saints. The six angels are chosen from the New Testament—four from the Gospels, two from the Revelation.

John Hutton's technique has developed enormously through the years. The angels he engraved for the Air Force Memorial at Runnymede were, I felt, too tightly drawn for Coventry and after

49

discussion he started a series of experiments that have gone on for five years.

His method now is to draw the figures with a turning wheel which can be varied by using different sizes and hardness. The effect is a spontaneous drawing, like chalk, of great vitality and expression, giving the exact feeling required.

This screen was a considerable challenge. Through it the visitor from the old Cathedral gets his first view of the altar. Although it may be difficult to see right through in the daytime, the effect at night should be exciting and I am certain that this screen will prove to be one of the great works of the Cathedral.

John Hutton's glass cannot be divorced from the bronze framework. This was in itself a most difficult structural problem as a sheet of glass 70' × 45' requires great stiffness to withstand the strong winds that will surely blow.

As usual, Ove Arup was fertile with ideas. A very simple solution came to him. The screen is hung from the roof and stiffened by making tie rods which are clearly visible from the porch and nave. The whole screen was most beautifully carried out in bronze by John Crittall's boys at Braintree, chief amongst them being Mr. Bunn, who is that rare combination of patience and tact.

The appointment of the stained glass artists was not so easy. The designing and making of the ten nave windows which rise about 75 feet from floor level to the ceiling is, I believe, the largest single commission for stained glass in the history of the craft. Normally stained glass is left to the last, almost as an afterthought, but, as will have been appreciated from my descriptions, at Coventry it is an integral part of the conception and an essential architectural element.

I had seen very little stained glass in this country that had excited me. The sort of thing going into our great cathedrals and Westminster shocked me to the core. The true English tradition of stained

27. *The lower lights of the Green Nave Window by Keith New. The polished black marble floor reflects the highlights and contributes towards an impression of magnitude in the interior.*

28. *Looking up at the multi-coloured, 72-foot-high Nave window by Geoffrey Clarke, the afternoon sun throwing its coloured light over the coarse texture plaster wall surface.*

glass can be seen at Fairford, Winchester, York and other places that have old glass of the thirteenth, fourteenth and fifteenth centuries. It is virile and strong; none of this wishy-washy stuff with sweet faces and poor realistic drawing.

I felt strongly about this for, during the war, I was attached with a small British Unit to General Patton's Army which liberated Chartres. After the excitement, the cheering, the speeches from General de Gaulle, I took my Commander and Major Paynter to see the Cathedral, for although they were not too keen I insisted it was a matter of duty to see this great Cathedral with its beautiful sculpture and glass, especially as we had helped to save it for posterity.

Alas, the sculpture was sandbagged right up and all the glass had been taken out and stored. The Cathedral was cold and dead— like a head without eyes; and I resolved that if ever I built a cathedral it should have singing breathing windows. Moreover, I would see to it that the glass was commissioned in good time and not left to the end, for if there was a financial crisis the first thing to be skimped on would be the glass.

But the choice of artists was difficult. I collected photographs of the work of the established stained-glass artists and discussed the situation with the Bishop, Provost and the Reconstruction Committee; and on a visit to the Royal College of Art, I came across some glass by two young students, qualified and on scholarships, that excited me beyond measure. The two were Geoffrey Clarke and Keith New, both students of Laurence Lee.

I discussed the matter with Robin Darwin, their Principal, and suggested that the Reconstruction Committee could enter into a contract with the Royal College of Art as contractors, who would employ Laurence Lee, Geoffrey Clarke and Keith New as their artists.

Obviously this was going to be most difficult to arrange. From the Committee's point of view I was recommending two completely untried and untested artists, although Laurence Lee was very experienced; and as custodians of public money the Committee were to commit about thirty thousand pounds to this venture.

I realised all this and told them so, but argued we must take a risk; we had to use fresh talent if we wished to return to the great tradition of English stained glass. It says a great deal for the Committee and its Chairman, Mr. Ford, that they took my advice and asked me to start negotiations with the Principal of the Royal College of Art.

With great difficulty Robin Darwin got the approval of the Ministry of Education and the other bodies interested in the Royal College (he is perhaps one of the few principals in England who could have pushed this through) and on the whole the arrangement worked out well, for the three artists never failed to consult me and we worked most happily together.

I had given them the broad outline of my Competition report and stressed that I wanted modern windows, bright rich colours and strong design. I told them not to be inhibited, that I looked for the very best they could do.

The problem of the baptistry window still remained and I was discussing the problem one day with Hans Juda, the editor of *Ambassador*. He asked if I had seen John Piper's windows for the Chapel at Oundle.

I had not; but at once got in touch with John Piper and his collaborator, Patrick Reyntiens, and was shown the windows, still incomplete, in their studio near Henley-on-Thames. Piper had designed them and Reyntiens had interpreted the sketches into glass. I thought them most beautiful. As in the case of Fernand Lèger, who late in life turned to stained glass (his glass in the church at

Audincourt is an example), so I thought John Piper had found a new outlet for his genius.

Moreover, I felt that the right time to get the best from an artist in a new medium is to offer a real challenge when their invention is at its most fresh. Both Piper and Reyntiens were excited at the commission. The Committee appointed them and I started discussions with John about the design.

As this baptistry window is the only one to be seen as one enters the Cathedral, it is of vital importance. It is also very big, with 198 lights in all; even bigger than the great east window at Gloucester. As the tapestry was to be dominated by its huge figure of Christ, I felt it would be wrong to have any realistic representation in the window, and we therefore decided on a purely abstract design. John's design shows a pool of gold light hovering over the font, above the celestial colours, purple, ultramarine and other shades of blue; and under the pool of gold the earthy colours reach up—reds, green and dark brooding colours. The whole window is shot with streaks of very light or brilliant glass. It is a staggering design and to my mind a masterpiece.

CHAPTER 10

The Nave Develops

DURING MY holiday in Spain, I had kept saying to myself, 'It is going to be built, it is going to be built', over and over again—just to get used to the idea. I was exhilarated but critical. All the faults soon started to show themselves, like rats coming out of their holes, and certainly one of the elements of my design that appeared most full of faults was the vault.

The slow development of the nave was dependent on the design of the vault and the engineer, Ove Arup, was appointed early on (in 1951) to collaborate with me in its design.

Born a Dane, and now in his sixties, Ove Arup is one of the most talented engineers in Europe. But one of his most endearing characteristics is that with all his technical knowledge he is willing to listen to anybody—even architects! In an instant he understood the object and the subtler meanings of the design for the Cathedral as a whole and he has been selfless in giving all he could to the design. It has been a constant joy for me as architect to work with him, work that became so enjoyable that it turned into play.

When I did the first perspective sketch of the vault my mind turned to methods of construction. Of course it could be done, anything can be done—almost. Yet I felt there was no strong structural idea behind it; it was a decorative canopy, yet part of the roof structure.

So I decided to separate the vault from the actual roof of the building. This pleased Ove and allowed him to tackle the two

29. (above) *A fragment of the Baptistry window stained glass designed by John Piper and carried out by Patrick Reyntiens.*

30. (below) *The zig-zag plan turns the Nave windows towards the High Altar. Here are the lower portions of the windows by Lawrence Lee (left) and Geoffrey Clarke (right).*

structural problems separately: the roof which would protect the building against the climate, and the vault which was a piece of furniture free from the side walls and upper structure. It was held only at the east end over the tapestry and at the great glass screen.

He and I spent many hours discussing the actual spacing of the vault supports, within the discipline of our grid, which was taken from the old Cathedral. This grid was reduced slightly and mathematically towards the altar, as I wanted a subtly tapering nave to concentrate attention on the altar.

We turned our gaze first on the column which would have to support this vault. Ove was not satisfied that the loads were balanced, as I had two rows of columns defining the aisles, so that the columns nearest the windows supported only half the vault. I just could not see how this would ever work well.

Then Ove got an idea; it was that each column should support a square mushroom of concrete and that there should be a linking area over the centre, on the main axis of the Chapel of Unity and the font. This was the solution and the grid remains unaltered to this day. Though the idea seems simple and obvious it was hard to find and demanded a great deal of thought.

The actual form of the vault went through many stages. The competition idea was for great plastic forms which would have to be cast against an expertly made wooden mould. This would be expensive and, as I already knew, was not flexible enough from the acoustical point of view.

I sought to break up the surface and my next suggestion was a form of geodetic construction like the structure of the fuselage of a Wellington bomber. Ove did not like it as it would be very expensive; but the ribs reminding one of the Gothic vault, coincided exactly with our diagonal grid lines. The columns were now a four-pointed star instead of the rather formless column that I had first suggested. Things were moving but there were many more snags.

I was struggling with this method when I saw in the *Geographical Magazine* a highly magnified photograph of a fly's eye. This was marvellous, with the most amazing facets and a compelling organic crystalline quality about it. It was the sort of thing I had already done in the baptistry window and other parts of the Cathedral, so after discussion with Ove it was decided to adopt this. (Later the *Daily Express* called it the 'Fly's Eye Cathedral'.)

Up to this stage the columns were perfectly regular and had parallel sides straight up their 60-odd feet. Now we decided on a taper coming down to a narrow section at the base, thickening where it hit the vault structure. This seemed logical enough, as the vault was like a great table with fourteen legs pushed into the Cathedral and many tables have tapered legs.

We discussed the junction of the column with the floor of the nave. Of course it could simply rise from the marble floor; but I was not happy with this as marble is such a different material from concrete. I felt that there should be some element to divorce these two materials so different in character.

Ove calculated how many tons were coming down each column and found it to be surprisingly small. Many different ideas were put forward and at last someone, it may have been Ove, suggested glass. 'Yes,' I shouted, 'glass spheres—transparent—that would be wonderful'; and Ove replied, 'and I shall order the goldfish!'

But alas, when we approached the glass companies they could not guarantee a life of 500 years for these glass feet and we had to abandon the idea. Now I see great radio pylons with insulators of some transparent material at their base; but we had ordered bronze pins and it was too late to change back.

This crystalline vault, supported by fourteen pillars, began to look like the final answer. But later when we had to make savings it was amended—and further improved. However, I felt dissatisfied with the way it bumped into the tapestry wall behind the High Altar. I liked the freedom of the sides and over the font and I searched for freedom over the altar. Then the obvious hit me. Why not remove the wall behind the altar and place the tapestry at the end of the Cathedral, cut out the 'East Window' to the Lady Chapel, light the tapestry with clear glass—and get a free standing High Altar with a reredos?

For a long time I had been worried by the proximity of this powerful tapestry to the altar where the intimate ceremony of Holy Communion would take place. Now this criticism was answered; the reredos would give that intimacy near at hand and the Cathedral would have another traditional English architecture—length.

I consulted Graham Sutherland, as this would alter his conditions. He agreed, and I also got the approval of the Provost, who thought it a great improvement, as did the Bishop and the Reconstruction Committee. I did a large perspective drawing and submitted it for the 1953 Summer Exhibition at the Royal Academy; it was hung in the central position of the Architecture Room and I was elected an A.R.A.

CHAPTER 11

The Tapestry Develops

SOON AFTER my visit to Villefranche, Graham Sutherland was appointed to design the tapestry. I do not think that more than one or two of the Committee knew his work and the reaction of some of them, including Mr. Ford, the Chairman of the Commitee, to the exhibition of Sutherland's work held at the Tate Gallery at that time, was stunned incomprehension. They seemed unable to make head or tail of it and when they spoke to me about it their eyes said, 'Let it be on your head'. But I assured them that he was an artist of enormous range. He could do abstracts, lyrical landscapes, imaginative compositions, portraits and great religious paintings like the Crucifixion at Northampton. 'Rest assured,' I said, 'he will react in a sensitive way to the problem.'

I knew he had grasped the first architectural essential, scale, for as he did not read plans easily I had a little model of the interior made to very small scale and had seen one of his first sketches in position there; I knew his conception of the tapestry would be a success.

But then we ran into great technical difficulties over the actual weaving. We had an unofficial liaison with the Edinburgh Tapestry Company* and by then I had had many discussions with Lady Jean Bertie and her husband about the weaving. But the situation here was difficult, for the Tapestry Company was running at a loss and was only kept going by the Berties, who knew I had faith in them and that if they wove the great tapestry the Company would become a

---

* Not to be confused with the Edinburgh Weavers.

31. *One of the Tablets of the Word. The incised lettering and symbols are by Ralph Beyer. Coloured light from the Red Window by Lawrence Lee is projected over the inscription by the sun.*

flourishing concern. They were willing to build a loom especially for this commission and to alter their studio at Corstorphine on the outskirts of Edinburgh.

Graham Sutherland knew their chief weaver, Ronald Cruickshank, well—he had interpreted Graham's wishes beautifully on the 'Wading Birds' tapestry—and was anxious that Cruickshank should be in charge of the weaving.

Both Lady Jean and Cruickshank wanted to do some trial pieces and the method we had decided was, I think, a good one. The artist's cartoon was drawn quite small, about the size of a large door, and was photographed up to the actual size of the tapestry. The photographs were to be the working drawing, so to speak, while the actual cartoon, a painting, would be used for the colour. The Edinburgh Tapestry Company were pleased with this scheme, as it gave their artist-weavers a creative hand in the weaving and I knew that this would give the vitality I wanted. Besides, the task of making a cartoon seventy feet by forty feet would have been a formidable one.

After some delay Graham did some sketches of the Calf, one of the Four Beasts, and I suggested that a sample should be done of this, although Graham was more intent on testing the weavers with a piece of drapery to see if they could interpret his colours and subtleties of drawing.

However, the Calf was woven and it was a shocking attempt. Not only was the drawing bad, but the colours did not match the sketch. Graham came up to Edinburgh to see it and hated it. The reputation of the artist rests in the hands of the weavers where a tapestry is concerned and there was disappointment and friction all round.

Although Graham was working on many sketches, he had not made up his mind on a first cartoon even by 1953. I can understand this as one cannot hurry a large commission of this kind; but the Edinburgh Tapestry Company was keeping going only in the hope of the Coventry Tapestry and the delays and difficulties were fatal. The Company went into liquidation and was taken over by John Noble. Cruickshank had resigned and a new artist-weaver, Saxe Shaw, was appointed.

Saxe Shaw had been to Paris and studied tapestry weaving at the Gobelin Ateliers, coming under the influence of Lurcat, who had a highly personal approach to tapestry design. He and Graham met and I was most uneasy; there was too much talk of 'interpretation'. It was decided that a trial should be done of one eye of the figure of Christ, taken from the first cartoon to be submitted to the Reconstruction Committee and Cathedral Council for their approval.

But alas, the sample weaving of this eye was a disappointment to Sutherland. Other samples, much more detailed, were woven, although the Tapestry Company said that if this degree of interpretation was required the price must go up. But the detailed eye was now much better and more what Graham Sutherland was looking for.

And now the crisis came with the Edinburgh Tapestry Company. They suggested the tapestry should be woven in separate pieces, about fifteen, and then stitched together. The weave they advocated was a coarse one of four or five stitches to the inch. I advised the Reconstruction Committee that this was not the sort of tapestry I had in mind. Graham and I agreed it must be woven in one piece and must be a finer weave in order to get the subtleties of colour and drawing.

A secondary consideration, but an important one, was that of interpretation. Graham had already had some misgivings; and of course a tapestry cannot be judged until it is finished, when it may be too late to rectify matters. The artist's reputation would be in the balance, as Sutherland confirmed by seeking out Madame Cuttoli in Paris, who had commissioned the tapestries we saw in Antibes in 1951 and who knew every weaver in Aubusson.

The Reconstruction Committee paid the Edinburgh Tapestry

Company for the work they had done and we started negotiations with a firm in Felletin near Aubusson, Pinton Frères. They were given a sample to weave; it was perfect. For the first time Graham was delighted and I could at last envisage a tapestry hanging on the 'East' wall of the Cathedral. Moreover, the price was less than that of the Edinburgh Company and they could weave it in one piece with twelve stitches to the inch for they already possessed a loom 12 metres wide.

Another technical question which had concerned me was that of the fastness of the dyes, and I knew that the dyes used by Pinton Frères with the waters of the Creuse at Aubusson had the test of time behind them.

An appointment was arranged in Paris to meet Madame Cuttoli, to discuss all details, and we met this gracious old lady in her drawing-room, which is hung with one of the most impressive collections of Picassos I could possibly imagine. She told me she had bought some of them for a few francs when Picasso was a struggling artist in Paris and she is still firm friends with him. She also showed us her collection of modern tapestries woven under her direction: great pieces by Rouault and Matisse, Picasso of course, Dufy, Leger and two superb ones, quite small and in very fine stitch, by Braque. I particularly envied her these last two.

Now our weaving problems seemed solved and we were ready to go; but Graham had second, or rather third, thoughts about the design and the third cartoon was produced.

In a way I am glad of this for later I ran into contractual and price difficulties and had to make considerable savings. One of these was to cut out the stone in the interior and substitute a hard pumice-like plaster (correct for acoustics at last) of pure white. This, of course, gave Graham the colour that he preferred for the interior but it meant completely recasting the colour range.

To my mind the final tapestry design is the best. It had the experience of the others behind it, the colours are magnificent and the design stronger, as the whole has a background of rich bright green going right down to the floor of the Lady Chapel. The central figure of Christ, dignified and majestic, is in tones of white and has a beautiful head, itself five feet high; and as I have said before, the beasts with their brilliant colours and imaginative design are unique in the history of this subject in any medium, painting, sculpture or mosaic.

At last Graham Sutherland and I met Monsieur Pinton and his son at Madame Cutoli's house in Paris. The son spoke perfect English and interpreted for his father who, with his bright blue eyes and quickness of manner, made an excellent impression. Monsieur Pinton's firm had eighty weavers at its disposal and a long tradition of quality handed down from father to son. I felt confident. The enlarged photographs were being printed and after a discussion about colours with Graham, the wool was ordered.

However, when my wife and I called at Felletin in 1958 on our way to Lake Maggiore to see how Pinton was getting on, he told me he was stuck; the full-size photograph had arrived but there were many parts that required Graham's decision and guidance and although M. Pinton had written to Graham he had received no reply. As I was now getting anxious about time, I ordered a trial piece of one of the beasts and told M. Pinton to do the interpretation, using the enlarged photograph for tone and line and the original painting for colour but without Graham's guidance on the spot. This he did, and produced a masterpiece.

Graham went over to Paris to see it and was delighted. This sample served its object: to get things started and show how good Pinton Frères were even without help from the artist. Graham Sutherland and Monsieur Pinton were able to work happily as this sample piece of tapestry bred confidence between them and the full-size tapestry was started on 1st June 1959.

It is not generally known how difficult was the task M. Jean Pinton and his weavers accepted so cheerfully.

We were breaking all records in tapestry weaving in size and weight, and it must not be forgotten that the method of weaving was the traditional one, and the loom itself was over 500 years old, composed of two great tree-trunks weathered into gentleness by time. How fortunate that this, the longest tapestry loom in the world, *happened* to be the right length with only six inches to spare! The task of the weaver is to match the artist's design and colour in terms of woven wool, and if there are subtleties in tone, colour and drawing the weave has to be a fine one. The usual is about twelve stitches to the inch, which is the one in our tapestry. Sutherland's design is full of subtleties and the translation of drawing and colour requires great experience and knowledge. It is easy to understand the necessity for a close liaison between artist and weaver. A tapestry is composed of a warp and a weft. The warp is the structural part and must be robust as it is round these strong threads that the coloured wool weft is woven by the nimble fingers of the weavers. The warp is rolled on to one great roller and is slowly transferred on to the second after the coloured wool weft is woven on. One can realise that only a small part of the tapestry can be seen at one time, and the designer cannot get an idea of the whole until the end when the tapestry is cut off the loom. It is necessary therefore that the artist should be in constant attendance.

The method I suggested was to photograph a comparatively small painting (7' × 4') and then to enlarge it ten times by photograph. This relieved the artist of the arduous task of making a full-size cartoon for the weavers to work from, but at the same time kept the vigour of the smaller painting, as I was certain something would be lost in the translation from small to large if done by hand.

The weavers used these photographs for establishing the drawing and tone, but the colour was derived from the original painting. Here the fabulous colour sense of these French weavers is seen. Practically every subtle nuance was transferred from the painting to the tapestry, using thousands of different colours all specially dyed in the small vats beside the River Creuse whose waters, being alkali free, are ideal for fixing the dyes. The artist had to go over every foot of the enlarged photographs and make corrections and improvements as he thought fit. Fortunately, M. Pinton was so used to working for French artists of the calibre of Picasso, Braque and Leger that he understood the problem and he tackled this great task with verve and confidence. Only the future holds the results of this great adventure.

Unhappily, the only unsettling element in the long and sometimes tense story of the tapestry came at the end.

About five months before the Consecration, the Reconstruction Committee heard that there was a move to have the tapestry exhibited in Paris before delivery to the Cathedral. Later on it became clear that arrangements had been made for a possible exhibition in La Sainte-Chapelle.

The Committee met to consider this and as the tapestry would be completed in February it gave little time for such an exhibition. This tapestry weighed almost a ton and had to be hung most carefully as damage could easily be caused with such a heavy weight unevenly distributed. Furthermore, the organ builders required a month at least for tonal tuning after the tapestry was hung; and moreover the Provost wanted the Cathedral for rehearsals early in April.

Permission was refused, and Sutherland wrote letters, sent lengthy telegrams, gave interviews to the Press, generally raising the dust.

The Tapestry Develops

He complained that he was denied the opportunity to examine the tapestry properly before delivery to Coventry. In my opinion, it could only be finally judged in its designed position in the Cathedral itself, certainly not in La Sainte-Chapelle with its purple and blue glass giving a bluish light; for in the Cathedral I had been careful to introduce a large area of clear glass expressly to shine on the tapestry, so as not to distort the artist's colour balance.

Had it been possible for him to control the time-table better and thus leave more time at the end, the Committee and clergy might well have been more sympathetic to his proposal. I certainly would have supported his wish to hang the tapestry first in France but in a more suitable place than had been planned.

Nevertheless, this trouble, after ten years of negotiation, coaxing, worrying and in the end, we hope, triumph, cannot dim the sense of achievement and high adventure that attends all the works in the Cathedral.

THE CARTOON FOR THE TAPESTRY DESIGNED BY GRAHAM SUTHERLAND

THIS REFERS TO THE MAIN THEME OF THE TAPESTRY

"And immediately I was in the spirit:
and, behold, a throne was set in heaven,
and one sat on the throne.

And he that sat was to look upon like a
jasper and sardine stone:
and there was a rainbow round about the
throne in sight like unto an emerald. . . .

And in the midst of the throne,
and round about the throne, were four
beasts. . . .
And the first beast was like a lion,
and the second beast like a calf,
and the third beast had a face as a man,
and the fourth beast was like a flying eagle."

—Revelation IV, vs. 2, 3, 6 an

THIS REFERS TO THE DRAGON IN THE CHALICE UNDER CHRIST'S FEET

"Then another sign became visible in the sky
and I saw that it was a huge red dragon. . . .
Now they have conquered him through the
blood of the Lamb."

—Revelation XII, vs. 3 and
(J. B. Phillips' translati

THIS REFERS TO ST. MICHAEL HURLING DOWN THE DEVIL (ON THE RIGHT)

'Then war broke out in Heaven.
Michael and his angels battled with the dragon .
so the huge dragon, the serpent of ancient time
who is called the devil and Satan,
the deceiver of the whole world,
was hurled down upon the earth. . . ."

—Revelation XII, vs. 7, 8 an
(J. B. Phillips' translati

32. *Graham Sutherland's cartoon for the Tapestry, from which the weavers worked, is seven feet high. The Tapestry itself is 72 feet high.*

CHAPTER 12

St. Michael, Patron Saint, and Epstein

THE NEW Cathedral, like the old, is traditional in the sense that it shelters under one roof many branches of art.

Britain has never really excelled in the visual arts. Until recently she has not produced a sculptor of world stature, but although many here do not appreciate it, we now lead the world in this art. Our young sculptors take the highest prizes in the world's competitions, producing works of great imagination (it is a pity that they get so little support and that their efforts are not more recognised by the general public), and this abundance of talent is due mainly, I am certain, to two men of genius, giants in the world of sculpture: Sir Jacob Epstein, who was born in 1880 and died in 1959, and Henry Moore, much younger, born in 1898. It is they who have ploughed two lonely furrows and their followers, like seagulls behind the plough, have fed on their efforts. To my mind these two masters represent opposite points of view. Henry Moore, a deep and sensitive thinker, with the mind of a classical Greek sculptor, turned to stone for his greatest creations, while Sir Jacob felt profoundly and emotion flowed through his fingers into the clay as he moulded it. For me, he can muster in one piece of sculpture feeling as strong and spiritual as those embodied in the sculptures in the great mediaeval Cathedrals.

As with all the arts in the Cathedral, I gave much thought to the subject of sculpture and sculptors.

We were of course searching for someone who could do justice to the great figure of St. Michael, the Saint of our Cathedral, and I

67

had planned that the group should be twenty-five feet high from the base of the dragon to the top of the wings. I discussed the problem with Bishop Gorton, himself an amateur artist with strong views. He knew and suggested many reputable people, but yet we hesitated. The sculpture would be of such enormous importance to the Cathedral as a whole that we felt we must find an artist who would understand not only the artistic and technical facets of the commission but also the spiritual. And then one day on a convent in Cavendish Square there appeared the Mother and Child group by Sir Jacob Epstein, a work which Robert Furneaux Jordon has called the most significant piece of sculpture to appear in London for hundreds of years.

In the autumn of 1954 I took Bishop Gorton to see it. Removing his hat, he walked gently out into the centre of the busy street, completely oblivious of the traffic, and stood looking up at this masterpiece. I had to direct the traffic round him like a policeman when the road is up.

The sculpture held a deep message for him and he responded instantly. I have often seen people remove their hats as they pass this great work and the Bishop said simply: 'Epstein is the man for us.'

In the winter of 1954 I had given the prizes and addressed the University students in the Town Hall in Birmingham and at a reception in the Art Gallery afterwards I had met the curator, Mr. (now Sir) Trenchard Cox, now in charge of the Victoria and Albert Museum. He had shown me a little of his collection and dominating one hall was Epstein's 'Lucifer, The Fallen Angel', a most powerful piece which exudes evil from every finger. Surely, I thought, if Epstein could portray evil with such forcefulness he could portray the opposite in St. Michael. In any case I wanted a bronze, which would have to be modelled in clay before casting.

When I mentioned Epstein to the Reconstruction Committee

there was a shocked silence, at length broken by the remark, 'But he is a Jew'; to which I replied quietly, 'So was Jesus Christ.'

However, after a good deal of discussion and delay I got permission to approach Sir Jacob to ask if he were willing to do the group for us and what his fee would be. During all these difficult meetings when there was so much division of opinion, I could always rely on the support of the Bishop, Provost and Sir Fordham Flower, who, as Chairman of the Shakespeare Memorial Theatre, understood artists and had a liberal and appreciative attitude to modern art. I cannot say how much is due to his sensitive support.

Sir Jacob was then seventy-six, a short man, thick set and strong, with an expressive face and lively kindly eyes (although they could flash daggers at times). He had marvellous workman's hands with short strong fingers, rather like those of great pianists. I had not met him before and liked him at once. He invited me to the studio lent him by the Royal College of Art for the Christ he was doing for Llandaff Cathedral and was anxious to have my opinion of this great figure, fifteen feet tall. It was another great religious work, the head superb, but I felt that some vertical lines on the drapery disturbed me. To my surprise he accepted my criticism immediately. Like all great artists, he was fundamentally a humble man who would listen patiently to anybody he respected. I have seen him take serious note of the words of a child of nine because, to quote Epstein, 'Through innocence you find truth.'

When I asked him if he would accept the commission to do the great figure of St. Michael, he answered, 'All my life I have wanted to do Michael. This is a great task.' I asked what his fee would be, saying that funds were low, and he quoted a ridiculously small figure, adding, 'If the Committee can't pay that, I shall reduce it.' But his first figure was agreed.

I reported back to the Committee but they felt that Sir Jacob was such a controversial figure that they must have the backing of the Cathedral Council for his appointment.

I presented the case and the meeting was a stormy one. The Bishop, Provost, Sir Fordham Flower and I all pleaded for Epstein's appointment. I also urged that he should be appointed immediately, as he was born in 1880 and a great sculpture such as the Michael required physical strength; Sir Jacob did not use assistants but did everything himself.

Opposition came as little surprise from a Midland committee. There was prejudice, fear and lack of understanding. They had not experienced, as I had, Epstein's kindness, insight and above all his great humanity.

At last by a majority decision it was decided that he should be commissioned to do a 'maquette' about eighteen inches high to be submitted to the two committees before going further. At least we had a foot in the door.

Of course I did not give Sir Jacob all the background of this decision when I asked him to do the 'maquette', for it was really an insult to a sculptor of his eminence, but the Cathedral Council wanted the Provost to have a preliminary talk with him before the work was begun.

Lady Epstein invited us to lunch, and as it was a Friday the main course was fish preceded by a very nice risotto. It was a delicious lunch and the Provost got on famously with Sir Jacob, going into a long theological discussion on the significance of St. Michael, which led at last to delicate ground. The Provost asked the great sculptor what his beliefs were, and Epstein replied, 'My beliefs can be clearly seen through my work' (he pronounced work 'woik' as he never quite lost the American twang of his youth). This answer was acceptable and we all parted in great amity. As I drove the Provost to the station to catch his train back to Coventry he said, 'What a

33. *A detail of the Head of Christ from Sutherland's Tapestry cartoon.*

34. *The head of St. Michael, photographed in Sir Jacob Epstein's studio. The sculpture was modelled in clay and cast in bronze.*

35. *Epstein's sculpture of St. Michael and the Devil which stands sentinel at the Porch of the Cathedral and is adjacent to the Baptistry window.*

charming man, but what a bohemian household. Fancy starting lunch with rice pudding.'

There was an interval of several months before we communicated with Sir Jacob again, for he had promised to let me know when he had anything to show. In the interval Dr. Gorton died and a new Bishop was appointed. I felt the loss deeply as I had grown to love our Bishop; moreover I found solace and comfort and above all confidence and purpose after even a few minutes discussion with him. It was certainly fortunate for the Cathedral and for me that the new Bishop was Cuthbert Bardsley, for he turned out to be a real 'St. Michael', with all the fighting qualities of our Cathedral Saint. Like Dr. Gorton, he was deeply interested in all the arts and his hobby was to paint landscape in oils whenever he had a spare moment.

One day I read a newspaper paragraph quoting Sir Jacob as saying that the St. Michael for the new Coventry Cathedral was going to be his greatest work. I rang him up and asked him what was cooking. 'Come and see,' he said.

He was modelling St. Michael in the studio attached to his house in Hyde Park Gate, and as I went into this room crowded with plaster casts of busts of great men, beautiful women and children, I had another of the many shocks which attended the building of the Cathedral: not only had Sir Jacob done the maquette but he had started on the full-size figure. The head was done and he had roughed out the torso. It was magnificent, but I was perturbed. 'Sir Jacob,' I said, 'the Committee want to see the "maquette" and approve it before going on to the full size group.'

'Am I going too fast?' he asked; then after a moment added, 'Look, I'm not working for the Committee any more, I am working for myself.'

I telephoned the Provost and the Bishop and they came next day to see Sir Jacob and St. Michael. Without a moment's hesitation they both praised it. They said they wanted to see nothing else as the head was truly wonderful. Photographs were taken that day, an emergency meeting of the Cathedral Council and Reconstruction Committee was called in Coventry and Sir Jacob's work was approved —unanimously this time.

There was no hitch after this. Sir Jacob carried on steadily with the big figure and the devil. He worked in a small studio for such a big group and modelled it in pieces which, when completed, were sent away to be cast in plaster. He sometimes used very curious objects for supports; when he came to do the devil he used an old but solid kitchen table. It looked very odd to see a most evil devil twelve feet long with a kitchen table growing out of his backside.

The group was cast in bronze, which was not doctored in any way but left to mature in the open. Two years before consecration, we placed St. Michael on the Cathedral. Lady Epstein unveiled it, for Sir Jacob did not live to see the finished sculpture in position. During the ceremony I felt his presence.

It is a great emotional work which will be understood by all. I have heard criticism of the form but I know that the sculptor wished to communicate with the ordinary man, woman and child. He always placed this as top priority.

Just before Sir Jacob died he completed a bust of me for the Royal Institute of British Architects. Sitting for this gave me the opportunity to watch him at work and study his methods.

When I had telephoned him to ask if he would do the bust he seemed enthusiastic, but—'There is a snag,' I said. 'Money?' he asked. I told him the very small sums the Council allows for Presidential portraits and he remarked that it was about half his usual fee.

'We only want head and neck, Sir Jacob.'

St. Michael, Patron Saint, and Epstein

'Ah, that's good. You are best represented by head and neck. When I did Bernard Shaw he didn't agree to just his head and neck. He argued so strongly that I made an excuse and left the studio. When I came back he had taken off all his clothes and demanded my opinion. I said he was skinny.'

Sir Jacob completed my portrait in seven sittings. Starting with a lump of clay the size of an apple, he slowly built it up with successive layers, carefully moulding the form. It was wonderful to watch it grow under his hands, to the accompaniment of bursts of Hebrew or 'stay there', when he dabbed a lump of clay in position.

Sometimes he would work gently on an easy part and then he would discuss his youth and his early struggles in Paris, his friend the painter Modigliani who took hashish and who forced his drawings on unwilling buyers for five francs (drawings worth thousands today). Epstein saw people tear their drawings in half and throw them in the gutter rather than be bothered with taking them home.

Even though he had agreed to do only a head and neck of me, when he came to the point he said my head needed the support of shoulders which had to be without clothing, and he asked me to take off my shirt and then my vest. I felt shy as the caster and also his wife were in the studio removing the mould from a plaster cast.

Epstein saw my embarrassment and murmured, 'Don't be shy—you look just like a Japanese wrestler.' Small comfort, but he meant it kindly.

I have not mentioned before the series of bays worked into the old Cathedral which Provost Howard has called Hallowing Places. The idea was that men and women should worship through their various activities—as the Provost has put it to me on many occasions, 'To sanctify the activities and works of Man.' These bays represent Work, Healing, Teaching, etc., and though a theological controversy has always centred on these Hallowing Places they did have a purpose for the simple ordinary person who wandered round the old building.

As can be seen in Appendix B (pages 110 and 111) it was a Condition of the competition that they were to be included in the Cathedral plan.

I placed eight in the window recesses, with an ideal side light from the nave windows slanting across them. The fifth bay on either side of the nave was occupied by the organ.

On my competition submission I had represented these Hallowing Places as deep relief sculpture which I now came to dislike. I took advice from Henry Moore about them and he said that as we had not yet mastered the technique of relief sculpture, somehow it always looked banal. It was best to steer clear of it. He recommended freestanding figures.

But I found it impossible to show the purpose of these recesses with free-standing sculpture and I had long and earnest discussions with the Provost on the subject.

One day I was discussing the problem with Nikolaus Pevsner and considering a simple line incision—like Egyptian carving—when he suggested I should meet a young sculptor friend of his, Ralph Beyer, a son of Professor Oskar Beyer, the distinguished German who was a great authority on the incised lettering and symbols on slabs in the catacombs at Rome. He passed much of his knowledge to his son.

The idea appealed to me, for I thought that words, beautifully carved and in letters a foot high, might be the best solution, 'The Word' supported perhaps by a few simply incised symbols. In the past simple people entering the cathedrals to worship could read only with difficulty, while many could not read at all; but now with universal literacy the word had great meaning—more I thought, than indifferently carved pictorial panels.

Ralph Beyer is a diffident and humble person, though a most

sensitive carver of letters. He showed me the publication on his father's researches in the Catacombs. They were superb. The Provost agreed to the project and gave Ralph a suitable sentence to carve as a trial stone.

We agreed that the letters should not be stereotyped Roman or Gothic or any other letter but should be 'felt'—some irregular, some smaller than others, but each one a piece of incised sculpture in its own right. They would be carved letters, not printed, so that the sensitive irregularity of the letter panels in the Catacombs became a possibility for us.

Then came the great question: What words to carve?

By now the new Bishop had been appointed and although he had no objection to panels of incised lettering and symbols being embodied in the Cathedral, he did not like the phrase 'Hallowing Places'. Since then the Provost and everybody else has called them just 'the Panels', and latterly 'The Tablets of the Word'. A small committee of the Provost and Canon's Theologian decided that the Panels should present important aspects of Christian teaching and be a mirror of the Life of our Lord.

Here are the final wordings from the New Testament:

> I and the Father are one
> He that hath seen Me
> hath seen the Father
>
> The Son of Man is come to seek
> and to save that which was lost.
> The good shepherd giveth his life
> for the sheep.
>
> Come unto Me all ye that labour and are heavy laden
> and I will give you rest. Take My yoke upon you
> and learn of Me for I am meek and lowly
> in heart and ye shall find rest unto your souls.

75

Phoenix at Coventry

A new commandment I give unto you
that ye love one another
as I have loved you

I am the Vine,
Ye are the branches.
He that abideth in Me
and I in him
the same beareth much fruit
for apart from Me ye can do nothing.

When the comforter is come
whom I will send unto you from the Father
even the Spirit of Truth which proceedeth
from the Father he shall testify of Me
and ye also shall bear witness.

Whoso eateth My flesh
and drinketh My blood
hath eternal life.

Fear not
I am the first and the last
I am alive for evermore amen
and have the keys of hell and of death.

These phrases represent many months of patient work and thought, for it is not easy to compress Christ's message into eight stone panels in phrases which will strike the attention of the casual as well as the devout reader and remain—as they should do—in his memory.

On a sunny day at midday and two-fifteen in the afternoon, beams of coloured light slant across these panels. In this beautiful illumination the full poetry and meaning seems to come out of the Tablets of the Word, each letter carved with sensitive feeling.

CHAPTER 13

To North America

RIGHT FROM the beginning the design for the new Cathedral has been controversial. Though the Reconstruction Committee was solidly behind the design and we had always had the backing of the Cathedral Council, the Coventry City Council was strongly against it and many people had got into the habit of saying 'that concrete monstrosity' without knowing much about the design or indeed caring very much.

In the early days, the Reconstruction Committee felt that if public hostility to the design were maintained the Minister of Works might not grant a licence to build and the Bishop asked me never to lose an opportunity of talking about it to groups of people if I were invited.

So I accepted every invitation to lecture during the years 1952, 1953 and 1954 and continued to give some lectures in 1955, 1956 and 1957, although it was difficult to accept invitations in these last years as I was appointed Professor of Architecture at Leeds University and was also getting busy again in my own office. When I became President of the Royal Institute of British Architects I had to stop altogether, although on one recent Presidential tour of Africa I took the British Council film of the Cathedral and showed it many times, introducing it and answering questions afterwards.

It is amazing how the interest has kept up through the years; even now I get an average of two requests a week for lectures on the Cathedral.

In the three years after winning the Competition I must have spoken many hundreds of times; it was a common occurrence to accept three invitations a week. I went all over the country, from Aberdeen to the Isle of Wight. I visited many places several times, talking to different societies—sometimes to large audiences, as at Brighton when the Banqueting Hall in the Pavilion was crowded out, and sometimes to small groups of clergy, as at Rugby, or to public meetings of over a thousand or a handful of students in a school of architecture.

In many places—Lincoln for example—I found the atmosphere very hostile when I went in, but after I had told the whole story of the design, people came up and said they had quite changed their views. These explanatory talks, I am sure, helped to wear down the hostility to the design and brought people to understand its purposes. These lectures exhausted me, but I knew they were important and was encouraged by the response. But in my heart I knew that any amount of talking would not alter the design; the building would have to speak for itself.

As I have said, I got no new commissions till well into 1954, so that when the Reconstruction Committee received an invitation from Canada, they asked me if I would accompany the Provost and the Bishop's Chaplain, Clifford Ross, on an appeal tour. Canada has been a great friend to the Cathedral. From the beginning Canadians gave donations and the Canadian College of Organists collected a large sum for the organ.

Clifford Ross went first, touring the whole of Canada and organising small appeal committees in practically every city of any size, together with a sponsor. He came back with a donation of two thousand pounds for a new travelling model of the Cathedral.

A beautiful one was made by Fred Keil's boys in City Display and towards the end of September 1953 the Provost, Ross and I set off with it to Canada by air for a three-months' trip.

To North America

After a ghastly night (we were travelling tourist) we arrived at Montreal airport, and although it was very early in the morning, we were met by the sponsors of the appeal in that city. The Provost and Clifford Ross were welcomed heartily, but a look of surprise spread over their faces when I was introduced. 'The architect? Why, he must be here for the ride,' they seemed to be thinking, and this proved to be their reaction all over Canada.

Perhaps it was the bad night and I was imagining things, but I felt very hurt. I was giving up three months when I ought to have been looking for work to keep my office going and I was doing this without fee; the Reconstruction Committee had offered one but I had refused.

I was even more hurt that afternoon when our sponsor, having had the model set up in Eaton's Store—a sort of Selfridges—suggested I should go on duty and answer questions. I asked if any lectures had been laid on. 'Do you lecture?' he enquired blandly.

That evening I asked Clifford Ross to book my passage home. I felt it was all a waste of my time and the Cathedral's money. He took me to the hotel bar, gave me a glass of whisky, and another. He begged me not to go back.

He is a persuasive talker. I stayed and never really regretted it, even though my feelings were still sometimes ruffled. Once, for instance, I was on duty answering questions when a tall, formidable lady in a Queen Mary toque said, 'Young man [sic], what is the meaning of that radio pylon on the roof of your building?'

'That, ma'am, is a flèche.' She looked puzzled so I added, 'A flèche is a spire-like structure that in many countries, especially in France, is seen on the crossings of the great cathedrals.'

She was not satisfied. Pointing at it, she said loudly, 'I advise you to remove that radio pylon. What use is it, anyhow?'

A crowd had collected by now, so I drew myself to my full height and answered, 'Ma'am, it is there to receive the messages from Heaven.'

Although Montreal is mainly a Roman Catholic city, peopled as it is by French Canadians, it was by far the most successful from the appeal point of view. E. J. Maconnell, a great philanthropist and a Free Churchman, gave five thousand pounds to start the ball rolling, others followed his example and the ordinary citizen, seeing the model, gave generously—far more than other cities which were mainly Protestant.

In Toronto, for example, the wealthiest city in Canada, the appeal was not nearly so successful and many Scots there told me they would have donated if it had been a Presbyterian church.

The tour gained momentum: to Quebec to have tea with the Governor-General, Vincent Massey, a charming person; to London and Windsor, Niagara Falls, Detroit.

I was smuggled into United States territory in the company of six Canadian clergymen, as my visa for the U.S.A. had not come through. I wanted to see Cranbrook, a fascinating 'university' built on the whim of the American millionaire George Booth in 1928. It comprised a complex of buildings superbly designed and laid out by that great Finnish architect, Saarinen, who left Helsinki and became an American citizen. His son Eero, who has just died at the age of fifty-one, carried on the tradition and was one of America's most distinguished architects. Saarinen senior had been professor of architecture at Cranbrook, and the professor of sculpture was Carl Milles, the Swedish sculptor whose work adorns many public buildings in Stockholm (he too became an American citizen) and Cranbrook simply oozed with his sculptures. The place was a 'Shangri-La' of a university with porticos, pools and fountains lavish with Milles' sculpture, rich in flowers and with an art gallery in which there were works ranging from the Italian masters to Henry Moore.

Then on to Winnipeg, where the professor of architecture at the University, John Russell, asked me to lecture to his students. They wanted the whole story—no time limit. I spoke for an hour and three-quarters and they asked questions for a further two. I was invited back three more times to lecture to groups of students of the other faculties in Manitoba University. The students made a spontaneous collection and raised several hundred dollars. This was the sort of response that made the trip worth while.

At Calgary, famous for oil and beef, we stayed at the Ranchman's Club—a highly select establishment—and when I was introduced to an important member there, he said, 'So you're the perpetrator of that concrete monstrosity.' Fame of a kind spreads fast!

I had been asked to lecture to 'The Imperial Order of the Daughters of the Empire' (I.O.D.E.), the most energetic women's society in Canada. The I.O.D.E. had hired a wooden hall that could hold about eight hundred people and it was almost full. I was ushered into a room by the handsome Canadian lady who was chairman of the meeting and introduced to my bodyguard of twelve very good-looking ladies all dressed in white flannel suits with white berets and shoes. Each was armed with an enormous Union Jack. To the strains of 'Land of Hope and Glory' I was processed on to the platform, finding it difficult to keep step, as it was played at a deadly slow tempo.

I was introduced by the Provost, gave my lecture, then invited questions, and during question time I noticed whisps of mist creeping into the hall under the doors.

Now, Calgary is at the foothills of the Rockies and I knew that it occasionally enjoys a meteorological freak called the 'Chinook'—a warm wind that can increase a temperature of forty below to forty above in fifteen minutes. So when I saw the creeping mist I thought, 'Ah ha—Chinook'. I noticed, too, that queerly clad people, mainly women, were moving in and occupying the few spare seats at the back of the hall. As I wondered who they were, Madam Chairman whispered to me that unfortunately she must end the meeting at once. She rose and said, 'Friends, I deeply regret I have no alternative but to call this most interesting meeting to a close. All I can say is that Mr. Spence has burned us all up.'

Then I discovered that the building next door was on fire and the flames were threatening our hall. When we went outside the streets were crowded and firemen on ladders were rescuing people from the flaming building and sheltering them in our hall in their night clothes. Anything can happen in Calgary.

The miles mounted up. I remember the magnificent scenery of the train journey across the Rockies; and the notices displayed in a small hotel at Revelstoke where we stopped the night. In the foyer it was 'Do not Spit', in the bedroom 'Do not smoke in bed', and at the Reception Desk 'Receptionist on duty—Maisy'. (We collected over a hundred dollars at Revelstoke.) I remember Vancouver, with lectures and broadcasts and the glittering Pacific Ocean; then Toronto again to be guest at the St. Andrew's Day Dinner at which a remarkable oration by Leonard Brockington, a charming and brilliant Welshman married to a Scotswoman, was awarded a standing ovation from his Scots audience, most of which had tears streaming down their cheeks.

I also received an invitation to lunch with the New York architects and tell them about the Cathedral. The Provost and Clifford thought it worthwhile to see if New York was fertile ground for an appeal, so we had New York thrown in too. The New York architects were interested in my description of the Cathedral but they sat up and really took notice when I described the great tapestry

as being the largest in the world and more than four times the size of
their biggest.

The Canadians were generous and kind, but the poor Provost had
to tackle the big business men and ask them to donate—a horrible
job and he hated doing it. However, he never shirked it and stead-
fastly did his duty, which invariably gave him a severe stomach upset,
during which he had to go on bread and milk. But he found it
difficult to get the hotel staff to understand what he really wanted;
he was always given a jug of cold milk and a slice or two of bread.
Patiently and with precision the Provost explained that all he wanted
was a soup plate of warm milk with bread in it. Comprehension
dawned on the waiter, 'Oh,' he said, 'you mean graveyard stew.'
Thereafter when the Provost had more tycoons to tackle and yet
another tummy upset, he lifted the receiver and asked for 'Graveyard
stew'.

In many ways the trip was difficult for me too. I was pitchforked
into the ecclesiastical world of Canada, there was little rest for we
were constantly on the move and I was very worried about my business at home. But Clifford Ross was my guardian angel. He kept me
going with his cheerful humorous outlook warmed by a deep
Christian sympathy. (The Canadians called him 'the baby-faced
bandit'.) I used to discuss my worries with him and he said calmly,
'Don't worry, everything will be all right. I shall pray that you get
all the work you want.'

When we arrived home just before Christmas 1953 I found the
office in a turmoil. No work had come in and my partners did not
know where to turn with worry, for the bank wanted our overdraft,
now at five figures, wiped out in a fortnight. We had to sack our best
people—people we had trained since the War—but somehow we
scraped through those nightmare days and in about six months
things slowly began to improve. Then rapidly—so rapidly that it was

difficult to cope adequately with the influx of commissions to design universities, churches, schools and many other kinds of buildings.

About this time I met Clifford again. He asked anxiously, 'How is the business?' I told him and said, 'Clifford, are you still praying for work to come to me?' When he answered, 'Yes,' I said, 'Then for goodness' sake, please stop.' But as the work still flows in I am certain he is still at it.

Our Canadian trip was a rewarding experience not only for the Cathedral but for the many friendly contacts we all made during it. I know now it would have been a great loss to me if I had succumbed to my childish feelings at the beginning of the tour: I shall always be grateful to Clifford for his sympathetic wisdom. To mark our visit there and Canadian generosity, a copper maple leaf is being inlaid in the marble floor of the Cathedral.

CHAPTER 14

Licence, First Contract and Financial Crisis

IN MARCH 1955 we were ready to start building the foundations. We had the finance, we were eager to start, and an application for a licence was made to the Minister of Works, Sir David Eccles.

It is easy to forget how difficult it was as recently as 1954 to get a licence to build what was called an unessential building. Officially the Cathedral came into this category.

Unfortunately the project had never had the wholehearted backing of the Coventry City Council. Right from the beginning the majority of members of this body had used every device to delay and set obstacles in our path. They said that the Cathedral building would take bricks which were needed to build homes for the workers, although ours was a stone Cathedral without a single brick. They insisted on priority for a new Law Court and Police Station. Then that swimming baths would be preferred—cleanliness being next to godliness, of course.

A deputation from the Coventry City Council actually visited the Minister to oppose the granting of a licence on the grounds that the Cathedral was unnecessary. Apart from the aesthetic and religious aspects of the matter, they appeared to ignore the revenue brought to the city by visitors who come—and would continue to come—to visit the Cathedral.

This was all the more remarkable as the Coventry City Council were not responsible for the cost. The War Damage Commission paid the majority and public subscription the rest. Up to the moment of writing, the Coventry City Council has not voted one penny towards the funds and they are making little or no effort to clear the immediate surroundings in time for consecration.

I have often puzzled over some particularly spiteful attack on the design by a member of the Coventry City Council. It may be that the building project has always had the glare of publicity and in the job of vote catching, criticism of the Cathedral may play a part. I have even noticed latterly that some councillors have had to resort to praise, even though luke-warm.

Although I have found the attitude of the Coventry City Council incomprehensible, I have nothing but praise for their permanent officials. These helpful and sagacious men took an objective view; and as for the Architect, Donald Gibson, I can truly say that without his help we could not have even started. His position was extremely delicate but I could always rely on his help. Unfortunately, he found it necessary to leave Coventry and go elsewhere, but the tradition he began was faithfully carried on by his successor, Arthur Ling.

However, despite all difficulties and opposition, and despite the fact that licences for building were suspended, a fortnight after our application and the Minister could therefore have delayed, a licence was issued—an historic document, unique and perhaps both the first and last of its kind. I reproduce it.

The issuing of the licence was accompanied by a letter from Sir David to the Lord Mayor of Coventry. It is dated the 28th April 1954. Here is an extract:

'The Cathedral is not a building which concerns Coventry and Coventry alone. The echo of the bombs which destroyed your City was heard round the world. We cannot tell how many people are waiting in this country and abroad for this church to rise and prove that English traditions live again after the blitz. The threat of far

36. *The Chapel of Unity is set on the cross axis of the Baptistry. The battered walls are clad in riven slate. The Chapel is to be used for interdenominational services.*

37. *The interior of the Chapel of Unity has a dished floor of marble mosaic designed by Einar Forseth and donated by the people of Sweden.*

MINISTRY OF WORKS

C.L. 1138

Revised October, 1951

BUILDING LICENCE

Building Licensing—Defence (General) Regulations 1939
Regulation 56A

LICENCE No. :
9/0/141822

Please quote on
all correspondence

To. The Coventry Cathedral Reconstruction Committee,

22, Bayley Lane,

Coventry.

Ministry of Works,
Regional Licensing Officer,
Ashley Street,
BIRMINGHAM, 5

Tel. Midland 7121

SUBJECT TO THE CONDITIONS hereafter set forth, this LICENCE is hereby granted to carry out

building of new Cathedral

at......Coventry.

at a TOTAL COST not exceeding £985,000... (Nine hundred and eightyfive.....pounds)
thousand

in accordance with the APPLICATION dated...5th May, 1954.

and the ~~PLANS AND SPECIFICATIONS~~ Drawings submitted

(Date)......6th May, 1954.......... (Signed). William S. Allen

CONDITIONS on behalf of the Minister of Works

One responsible person must be appointed to complete information on the
progress of the job, on Ministry of Works Form C.P.S.23, which is sent
out each month, and should be returned to Regional Programmes and
Statistics Officer as soon as possible after the last pay day of each
month.
The contents of this licence and of any documents relative thereto must
be made known to any builder, contractor, architect, engineer or other
person employed in an advisory or supervisory capacity in connection
with the work.

For further conditions and Notes, see overleaf

H

worse destruction is with us today demoralising and corrupting our thoughts. We have never had a greater need for acts of Faith.'

Now the Cathedral entered into a new phase of construction, although work had been progressing steadily all the time on the stained-glass windows of the nave and the old Cathedral walls were being repaired and made sound, slowly but thoroughly.

As the details of the superstructure and the vault were still being worked out, it was logical to start work on what was known to be firm and unalterable: the foundations.

The engineers had been toiling for many months on their detailed drawings and were ready. But how to select a contractor? The Reconstruction Committee decided to advertise for tenders making it clear that a selection would be made from the applicants.

The response was overwhelming and we eventually narrowed the final choice down to six, on a more or less regional basis.

The firm of John Laing (one of the best known, with an excellent reputation) submitted the lowest tender, but even on this point there were storms. Local representation pressed for the appointment of a small local contractor, who although good, was in my opinion not equal to undertaking a large civil engineering contract for Cathedral foundations. Every conceivable argument was put forward for their employment but I was adamant. I even told the Provost and the Chairman of the Reconstruction Committee, Mr. Ford, that I would rather resign than agree to the appointment of an unsuitable firm who were not even the lowest tenderer.

I had my way, and on the 10th January 1955, the contract was signed in Coventry between the Reconstruction Committee and Messrs. John Laing. Work started at once.

In the meantime I had selected a Clerk of Works who was duly appointed. Mr. Thomas John Hocking turned out to be a strong and faithful servant of the Cathedral project. I could rely on his support at all times for he was the first of many who fell under the spell of the Cathedral.

Now my attention switched to the final drawings for the super-structure, which included all the stonework and the vault in the nave. A second contract would be needed here, and I asked our surveyors, James Barr of Glasgow, for an accurate assessment of cost. The bulk of the superstructure was to be stone, a scarce material in immediate post-war building and therefore difficult to budget for, and in any case there was no precedent for a building of this kind. Barr's original forecast has been encouraging, but their latest findings came as a shock: in effect, that it would be unrealistic to expect the cost to come out much less than two million pounds.

This was terrible news as the War Damage payments and dona-tions, including the proceeds of our Canadian tour, amounted to little more than a million pounds and this was the limit. The foundations had been started, it would therefore be unwise and wasteful to alter them. The situation was desperate.

This was the back-cloth to a most difficult meeting of the Reconstruction Committee under its new Chairman, Sir Fordham Flower, Mr. Ford having died in 1954. Sir Fordham was a staunch ally of the Cathedral project. As I have said before, he understands artists and building problems and I was thankful he was in the chair when this financial crisis came.

As I was faced with the urgent need to cut expenditure, James Barr asked to be relieved of their position as Surveyors. They felt they were too far away in Glasgow to cope with the day-to-day problems, so Reynolds & Young were appointed in their place. I shall always be grateful to Bill Young and his partner Jack Osborne for their tireless help during the years that followed.

I looked to them for guidance, for somehow I had to cut the cost almost by half. I was deeply depressed and felt that only a miracle could save us. Radical alterations were now impossible, as work was well advanced on the site and in any case to decrease the floor area would seriously impair the function of the Cathedral. Other ways must be found.

As I could not cut the volume of the Cathedral, could I try to reduce the quantities of more expensive materials such as stone?

At this time the interior of the Cathedral was planned in the same stone as the outside; this was very expensive, especially as we would have to build the interior walls with slots on the inner face to catch and trap the sound waves. The Chapel of Unity was also a very expensive little building in solid stone and the porch, too, appeared to have excessive 'fat'. I concentrated on these three items. The acoustic experts had always been worried about the use of such a hard material as stone for the inner walls. They would have preferred something which could be made to absorb sound so that the final effect on the ear would be like that of Durham Cathedral. They assured me that given time they could develop such a surface. Basically, it would be a hard plaster of rough texture, and almost white. I remember Sutherland's criticism of the colour of the interior, echoed by Piper and the stained-glass team. So we tried replacing the inner stone skin with concrete block and rendering with a rough-textured material. The saving in cost was encouraging, and I welcomed the alteration for another reason as well. I had just been visiting Liverpool Cathedral which has a pink stone interior. It had been a dull day and at midday they had to use artificial light. Our Provost was anxious that the interior of our Cathedral should not be dark and even though I had a large glass area in the windows, the stained glass was rich in colour and did not admit much light. Pale walls would help.

Next I completely redesigned the Chapel of Unity. I demolished the tall stone link between this chapel and the Cathedral, substi-

38. *The interior of the Chapel of Unity looking up at the stained glass set in concrete, by Margaret Traherne, alternating with clear-glass windows.*

tuting a very light link containing a lot of clear glass. This automatically cut out the vertical screen which separated the Chapel of Unity from the nave.

I planned the chapel itself in cast concrete, with a reduced ground area but with split buttresses divided by a strip of stained glass nine inches wide, the concrete covered with slate. The chapel would then contrast with the Cathedral, emphasising the idea underlying its conception; that christian unity was new, and separate from the established church.

The surveyors told me that this would represent a saving of about one hundred thousand pounds for the chapel alone.

Apart from this saving, I like the new design. It was stronger and the area of stained glass would cost the exact amount of money donated by President Heuss of West Germany. (Incidentally, by this alteration I had returned to the very first ground plan I ever drew of this chapel—the plan I completed within twenty-four hours of my first visit to the Cathedral.)

I turned my mind to the stained glass. I wanted something different from the glass in the Cathedral which though nearly abstract had recognisable symbols in it. I felt this glass should be entirely abstract as I did not want the many different denominations represented to disagree, which might result in endless arguments.

A friend had introduced me to a young woman artist, Margaret Traherne, who did excellent glass. I went to her studio and was struck by her talent, especially for thick abstract glass set in concrete. Surely here was the means of getting the Chapel of Unity windows designed and constructed.

So I redesigned the chapel to a restricted budget, using President Heuss' gift as a limit for the stained glass and with the cooperation of Margaret Traherne, the framework for her windows took shape; tall slits fifty-six feet high and nine inches wide. She agreed to use the thick glass giving the most intense and beautiful colours imaginable.

What a success the glass is! When the sun shines, beams of rich colour slant in, casting patches of rainbow richness on the concrete walls.

My attention now concentrated on the porch which was intended as a link between the old and new.

The old Cathedral with its lace-like walls and delicate enclosure would contrast greatly with the new building, which was bound to look solid even from the south. Aesthetically, the Porch should soften this contrast and be a true buffer between the two architectural characters, but I was not convinced that my design did this. I felt the Porch was too solid and that the design would be improved if I made it more open.

This is just what I did. I cut out great chunks of stonework and simplified the whole design, amending the steps and jutting them out free of the building.

Now I realised there was hope. With these alterations, and if we simplified the paving plan outside, left the finishing of the areas below the nave until later, omitted the Guild Chapel and the Christian Service Centre for the time being, we were there.

The Reconstruction Committee met, considered these proposals and decided to adopt them. The miracle had happened.

CHAPTER 15

The Foundation Stone and Second Contract

THE FOUNDATION CONTRACT went along steadily, although unforeseen difficulties did of course arise. One was the large number of bones and skeletons we came across. In one area we uncovered a communal grave containing many skeletons—some thought it was a plague pit. I got quite used to seeing workmen striking the pose of Hamlet in the graveyard scene; the only real difference was the language.

The winter of 1955-6 was severe and the nave platform had to be ready for the ceremony of laying the foundation stone planned for 23rd March 1956. The Queen had graciously accepted the invitation to lay the stone and the Archbishop of Canterbury would bless it. Invitations were to be issued to 2,000 people and a great responsibility rested on us for the completion of the first contract before that date.

After conferences with the contractors and much thought, I advised the Committee that we would be ready in spite of the frost and hard weather. Laings used braziers and every heating device imaginable in order to complete on time and they did, much to the astonishment of Captain Thurston, the Secretary of the Reconstruction Committee, who handled the arrangements for the Foundation Stone Ceremony. Unfortunately the Committee had not thought it possible to complete the whole platform and so fewer people had been invited to attend than would in fact have been proper.

March 23rd came, and all was ready. The Queen, the Duke of Edinburgh, the Archbishop and the usual Lords and Ladies in Waiting were met by the Provost, who showed them the old Cathedral and I then explained the new one from a model we had placed in the ruins.

I was given only five minutes for the explanation and to answer questions—too short a time really to explain a design which had the reputation of being radical. However, I did my best; the Queen was charming and the Duke stepped in with one or two questions. I was amazed at his grasp of the design and the technical implications of modern construction. There was no doubt he required considered and full answers. When I told him that the tapestry would be the largest in the world ($70' \times 40'$) woven in one piece and weighing three-quarters of a ton, he remarked:

'I hope that is not its only quality.'

'No, sir,' I said. 'It is comparatively easy to do a small tapestry of quality—to do a large one as good is a real challenge. This one will be very large and very good at the same time,' which was the best I could do in the circumstances.

So that the Royal Party could walk easily on to the platform, we had removed the tracery from the middle of the five windows on the North side—the same window I went to in 1950 when I had imagined the whole Cathedral. The waiting people got their first view of the Queen framed in this ancient archway before she stepped down to the platform, and as soon as she came into view every man, woman and child waved their programmes so that a surging sea of moving white rectangles suddenly appeared. The day was bright, but cold with a strong wind. To cover the platform we had designed a huge canvas canopy supported on one pole and pegged down at the corners. The wind blew so hard and the canopy flapped with such vigour that I felt certain it would collapse with disastrous results.

However, though there were anxious moments, it held together, and the whole ceremony went off without a hitch. Thankfully I felt that yet another chapter had been written, for hidden in the crevices of my mind I had the fear that the Cathedral would never be built. Surely now there was no turning back, and with renewed enthusiasm I tackled the next stage; the second contract.

We had our superstructure drawing ready and the surveyors gave us the reassuring news that we should not be spending more than our budget.

I thought it logical to extend the first contract to the second, for John Laings had been a great success—pleasant to work with, business-like and, of course, superb craftsmen. I struggled hard to get the Reconstruction Committee to accept this, for although Sir Fordham Flower approved, some members of the Committee felt that as guardians of public money we should go out to competition again. But I persuaded and argued and eventually it was decided to negotiate a second contract with John Laing.

Of course, I was delighted and telephoned the news to Maurice Laing. Next day I got a letter from him saying that his firm considered it a great honour to be entrusted with this work and that at the end of the job they would give all their profit back to the Cathedral. He asked me not to publish this decision as it would detract from the spirit of the gift. I hope the Laing family will forgive me for breaking that promise now.

CHAPTER 16

The Chapel of the Cross

PROVOST HOWARD had made the rebuilding of his beloved Cathedral his life work. He had been firewatching on the roof of the old Cathedral when the bombs fell during the night of the 14th November 1940, and he often told me that once he was certain that it would rise again he would retire. He felt that a younger man should take over in good time so that the Christian life of the Cathedral would be insured. This was an act of great sacrifice, for I knew that nothing would have given him more pleasure and sense of achievement than to see his dreams realised while still in control of the project, but he is a great Christian and retired as he had said he would, soon after the second contract was under way.

The death or retirement of key people is always disturbing. New brooms sweep clean. We were now with our second Bishop; who was like gold to me, and our new Chairman Sir Fordham Flower was a rock of stability, his friendly help always ready, and I was in constant need of it. Could I possibly be lucky a third time?

One day the Bishop asked me to show a friend of his the stained glass which was being made at the Royal College of Art and introduced me to a young clergyman, tall and handsome with a beautiful speaking voice. This was 'Bill' Williams, who later I heard was to be the new Provost.

Would the new Provost fill the vacuum left by that great man, Provost Howard, with his devotion to the new and the old Cathedrals? The years to come will decide the answer to this question.

The Chapel of the Cross

Soon after Provost Williams was appointed the Bishop invited us both to lunch at the Athenaeum to discuss an important and urgent matter. They wanted me to find space in the part of the undercroft already built for a chapel to seat 500 people. They both felt the need to form the nucleus of a congregation in the new Cathedral without delay.

I was a bit nonplussed by this; no part of the building was yet watertight, the contractors must have freedom of movement and nothing could be done without their agreement and, in any case, how could we pay for it?

But even as I spoke I was thinking that I could convert an area reserved for the chair store into a temporary chapel. There was room for an altar and choir and I could squeeze five hundred seats into it. Both the Bishop and Provost begged me to look into it and report back as soon as possible.

The scheme proved practicable and the contractors had no objection. But the cost of making watertight the nave floor above, of heating and lighting was high and I was given only a thousand pounds for it all. However, it was done, everybody helped, the contractors, suppliers, and even the architects.

This little chapel is known as the Chapel of the Cross. Geoffrey Clarke designed and made a remarkable altar cross based on the famous charred cross in the ruins, but I asked him to make this one shine with light and he incorporated lumps of crystal into its body. These radiate light in a most arresting way. We used some of the panels of stained glass stored ready for the upper chamber, and with white paint and a beautiful golden curtain given by the Bishop to hang behind the simple altar, the chair store is transformed. It makes a charming little chapel which has a faithful congregation, and there are always people in it.

One of the most moving ceremonies in the history of our new

Cathedral took place in this chapel when it was consecrated for use.

During the service, when the altar was being blessed, the old Provost carried in the naked flame from the altar in the crypt chapel in the old Cathedral. With great dignity he handed the torch to the new Provost, who slowly lit the candles on the new altar. As their light flickered into being we all knew that spiritual life had been transferred at last from the old Cathedral to the new.

39. *The boulder for the font brought from the Holy Land set on a bronze stem and backed by the rich colours of John Piper's Baptistry window.*

CHAPTER 17

Some Small Things

THIS CHAPTER IS devoted to the small things, the jewels in the casket, those little features that grow during the development of a design and that together give a building life and character and make it breathe: the font, the floor of the Chapel of Unity, the choir stalls, the little chapel for private prayer, the Chapel of Christ the Servant, and the high altar with its cross and candlesticks.

The Font

For the font, I first determined to get a simple boulder from Iona, but when I mentioned this to a friend Frankland Dark, who was an architect for some important schemes in the Middle East, he offered to get one from Bethlehem. This he did, through a chain of enthusiastic friends, Moslem, Jewish and Christian, who transported over both land and sea. This was a wonderful piece of organisation which cost the Cathedral nothing. The boulder is in its natural state, exactly as it was 2,000 years ago. Primitive, simple and eloquent, it stands as a symbol from the Holy Land, with the Baptistry window blazing behind it.

I was anxious that the original patina on the boulder should be kept and that the minimum should be done to convert it into a font. We had already constructed a drain that led into the foundations of the Baptistry window so the boulder had to be bored to connect with this.

I wanted a simple recess carved out of the top to hold the water for

Baptism and I suggested that a scallop shell should be our model of the form it should take.

Ralph Beyer is carrying out this idea and the font should be quite unique, echoing perhaps the fundamental primitive feeling that I experienced at Lascaux and Zimbabwe.

The Chapel of Unity Floor

The Chapel of Unity is plain, as plain as some of the early Christian churches, where usually elaborate designs were worked into the floor; logically, I think, because the eyes are as often looking down as up.

Even on my Competition designs, I had a star as the basic pattern to this chapel floor; but now we had little to spend. However, one day a dynamic character blazed into the Cathedral orbit: the famous Swedish artist, Einar Forseth, who designed and carried out the gold mosaic in the Golden Hall of the world-famous Stockholm Radhuset. Like a comet with a trail of fire he came into my house at Canonbury, said he had visited the Cathedral and wanted to do something for it. The Swedes would pay, he said. The Cultural Attaché from the Swedish Embassy and others were present. They were cautious and reticent, but nothing could restrain Einar. He would do an inlaid marble floor for the chapel.

A month later he appeared with a design and some full-size drawings which filled my entrance hall. A subscription had been started by Mr. Torsten Landby, a Swedish business man resident in London, with support from the highest in Sweden.

Einar's design, basically a star, contained the continents and the symbols of the evangelists, the Holy Spirit in the centre, all inlaid in marbles. Mr. Cecil Whitehead, who is responsible for much of the beautiful marble work in St. Paul's Cathedral, is carrying out the design.

Some Small Things

This floor is not enough for Einar, however, and he is making five stained-glass windows to be set at the top of the stair from the undercroft. These are his personal gifts to the Cathedral, their subject the bringing of the Gospel to Sweden from these islands.

The Choir Stalls

It is curious how ideas come and how the final pattern of the Cathedral is formed. The chance visit of a distinguished Swedish artist had its effect; an evening spent in Graham Sutherland's house determined the canopies of the choir stalls.

In Graham's sitting-room is a beautiful Welsh mirror with an elaborate thorn frame constructed to a geometric pattern. This gave me the idea for the choir stall canopies—a simple idea, I thought, but it has taken two years to develop.

I wanted two avenues of thorns surmounting the stalls as a prelude to communion. People would pass between them before kneeling down at the communion rail. It has taken many patient hours of discussion with Gerald Brasted, who has made them and my son-in-law, Anthony Blee, who detailed them, before the correct shape, weight and structure could be reached. This has been a difficult exercise as there is no precedent. The scale had to be right and then we had to find a means of making them stand up structurally. As I write, the first few thorns are in position. I think they are right. As people pass the stalls, look up at the altar and the tapestry behind, they may want to pray quietly away from the nave.

The Gethsemane Chapel

Near the high altar is the chapel for private prayer, the Gethsemane Chapel. It is very simple in character with a beautiful low ciment fondu wall by Steven Sykes. As the subject for this relief, the

Provost had given us the following passage from St. Luke's Gospel (Chapter 22, verses 43-6).

43. And there appeared an angel unto him from heaven, strengthening him.
44. And being in an agony he prayed more earnestly: and his sweat was as it were great drops of blood falling down to the ground.
45. And when he rose up from prayer, and was come to his disciples, he found them sleeping for sorrow,
46. And said unto them, Why sleep ye? rise and pray, lest ye enter into temptation.

The angel is interpreted as St. Michael, and the disciples asleep in the garden are on the right, surrounded by darkness. The background of the angel is gold leaf, and Stephen Sykes has used bits of glass, mirror, mosaic, cut crystal and other materials to give life and vigour to this wall. It is seen clearly from the first door under the Porch after climbing the steps and passing Epstein's St. Michael.

There had to be a screen to divide worshippers from the main stream of visitors. I designed a screen with the Crown of Thorns as the basic motif. As their gift to the Cathedral, the Royal Engineers at Chatham carried out my design faithfully and with faultless craftsmanship in wrought iron. Their little cypher can be seen on the left-hand side of the screen. People going into this chapel to pray may be reminded by the Crown of Thorns that giving and sacrifice is a short cut to peace and tranquillity of mind.

The Industrial Chapel

Right from the beginning, craftsmanship was to have a place in the Cathedral, for Coventry is predominantly an industrial town where craftsmen hold an honourable place. In the original we had a Guild Chapel and this developed into the industrial Chapel of Christ the Servant with an industrial chaplain to look after it and be responsible for the services there. The Reverend Simon Phipps has taken this chapel under his wing and in it we hope to set up all the

40. *The Cathedral in course of erection during 1951. This view is of the North end with the old tower end spire silhouetted in the distance.*

41. *The Golden Cross with the original Cross of Nails.*

42. *Looking up at the canopy of concrete ribs and slatted spruce. On the left are the clear windows which light the tapestry. The organ had not been installed on the organ platform (centre) when this photograph was taken in March 1961.*

old stained glass saved from the bombed Cathedral. This will be put back slowly, but to begin with the windows will be clear, the ceiling in gold leaf and the Cross, a gift of the apprentices of Coventry, will rise through a crown of thorns designed and made by Geoffrey Clarke. The central altar will be of English oak.

Besides being responsible for this crown and three of the nave windows, Geoffrey Clarke has designed the topmost symbol crowning the fleche, the cross in the Chapel of the Cross and is now working on the high altar cross and candlesticks.

The Nave Chairs

Five years ago I asked the Committee to appoint Professor R. D. Russell to design a chair for the nave of the Cathedral. There are few chairs that fulfil the wide needs of a church chair. Dick Russell was an obvious choice as I believe he is the best chair designer in this country—and how difficult it is to design this simple everyday article!

It was decided that our chair should be strong and simple, stackable and capable of lashing together in batches, to accommodate hymn and prayer books and a kneeler, to be beautiful and inexpensive—an almost impossible task.

Dick has worked for four years on his design—I think he has solved the practical problems and when it came to aesthetics I found that his chair, like a flock of birds, improved when seen in the mass.

His brother, Sir Gordon, has made them for us. They are an example in oak of the chairmakers' art.

The Lectern Eagle

One of the last things to be designed was the pulpit and lectern. I had worked with Anthony Blee for two years searching for the correct answer to these most difficult items.

It is sometimes not realised how difficult it is to design simple things well, or well enough for the Cathedral. Pulpits, in my opinion, fall into this category.

In the end we went for a simple hexagon made in bronze with no canopy as this element would tend to clutter the interior. And the lectern had to have the traditional Eagle.

Elizabeth Frink, that gifted sculptress, was to my mind an obvious choice. She designed and carried out a magnificent bird which looks as if it had just settled there after a long flight. She modelled direct in plaster and by inserting ordinary kindling in the standard six-inch lengths gave the effect of the feathers. These can easily be seen on the bronze casting. She also made the symbol of the Holy Spirit (a Flame) above the Provost's Stall and her Bishop's Mitre crowns the Bishop's Throne.

The High Altar

The High Altar is of concrete, hammer-dressed so that it looks rather like a chunk of rough granite. It is twenty-one feet long and we have so placed it that the priest can officiate facing the congregation. He has a clear space in front as we have made a Calvary of black marble immediately behind him, where the altar cross will be placed. This cross will be so designed that the original Cross of Nails, now in the ruins, will be incorporated. Similar crosses of nails made from the hundreds left in the ruins after the fire, can be seen in many Anglican Cathedrals in all parts of the world. Provost Howard has sent many crosses of nails abroad. The influence of our cross has been great. This is the theme. The future holds the secrets of this design.

The Sanctuary Candlesticks

One of the last embellishments asked for by the clergy was six tall candlesticks to flank the high altar, three on each side. There is a trap in designing these as the design could be really good or equally bad.

To keep up our standard at the eleventh hour was very difficult. It was a temptation to say, 'Six simple tubes,' but this attitude just would not do.

After much thought and talk with Anthony Blee we decided to ask Hans Coper to do them in pottery. Perhaps this may start something as I have not seen pottery candle-holders in churches. My aim was a strong robust object about seven feet tall in scale with the huge concrete altar. Obviously an ordinary design would look puny— this is the pitfall.

As I write now, early in the new year of 1962, we have little more than four months to go before the final consecration. The Cathedral is virtually finished; the fast-developing photograph in the tray of chemicals is getting clearer every moment. Yet I still have a feeling of uncertainty and, at the same time, hope.

My mind goes back over the eleven years of toil, frustration, hope and ecstasy. I think of all the people who have helped in this great adventure, some of whom I have not yet mentioned: Mr. Stocks, Laing's site agent who has worked faithfully for many years but whose grumbles could fill a lifetime; Mr. Howe, also of Laings, who is a great finisher, and the master mason Harold Ratcliffe who, with his labourer mate Mr. Brady, built the Baptistry window, surely one of the most perfectly constructed windows in England; all the back-room boys at the Uttoxeter quarries of Stanton and Bettany, who have laboured to give us the stone, cut to shape and delivered to site; Laurence Holloway, who did the marble floor and the panels of the vault; the coppersmiths and bronzefounders; the electricians and heating engineers; the carpenters and joiners; the plumbers; Mr. Grunau, a Coventry citizen, who gave the two oak crosses in the porch and the oak altar tops for the high altar and the Lady Chapel. He never failed us in an emergency. And last, but certainly not least, my devoted and hardworking staff who through the years have served the Cathedral project. They have come from all corners of the earth, Switzerland, Yugoslavia, Germany, Australia, New Zealand, South Africa, Canada and the West Indies, and most of them have now returned home. They perhaps may never see the Cathedral they have helped to create, but without them the Cathedral would not exist.

This then, is the band of men and women, labourers, artists and technicians, who came under its spell and have made it possible for this building to rise like a Phoenix from the ashes of destruction and despair. Sir Kenneth Clark, when he visited the Cathedral recently, said that it brought together for a moment in history the best skills and talent in our country.

And for myself? The Cathedral is still incomplete, there is still hope that for me the vision will in fact become reality. I have not yet seen the tapestry in position, the floor uncovered. I have not yet heard the resonance of boys' voices with the organ. I have not yet seen the slanting beams of ruby and gold fall on the altar during a celebration.

Perhaps it is better this way; perhaps reality can never equal the picture I see as I write and that I saw right at the beginning eleven years ago. But this picture persists, through swelling mists of turmoil and crisis.

My mind goes back to 1954 when Sir David Eccles wrote to the Lord Mayor of Coventry—'The threat of far worse destruction is with us today, demoralising and corrupting our thoughts—we have never had a greater need of acts of Faith'.

The new Cathedral Church of Coventry is our Act of Faith.

APPENDIX A

The Committees

1. The Reconstruction Committee was responsible for building the new Cathedral. They organised the Architectural Competition, appointed the Architect and entered into contract with the builders, engineers, artists and specialists. It is headed by a chairman and the membership is about 10 of lay and clergy—it is appointed by the Cathedral Council.

2. The Cathedral Council (Chairman the Bishop) runs the affairs of the Cathedral and has powers to examine and veto decisions of the Reconstruction Committee. This veto was defeated by a narrow majority when the appointment of Sir Jacob Epstein was considered by them *after* the Reconstruction Committee had approved his appointment to carry out the St. Michael group.

3. The Coventry City Council had no control over the building of the Cathedral, with the exception of granting planning permission. The funds were from the War Damage Commissions (who contributed just short of a million pounds) and the remainder came from public subscriptions and from various appeals (e.g. the Bishop's Appeal and the Canadian Tour). So far the Coventry City Council has not contributed anything; but it does of course collect rates from the Cathedral—the ground on which the Cathedral stands belongs to the Cathedral. Maybe in time the Council will overcome their antipathy, see the Cathedral's benefit to the City and make a contribution.

4. The Joint Council are set up by the Cathedral Council to

control the building and equipping and running of the Chapel of
Unity and Christian Service Centre. It is comprised of one half
Church of England and the other half members of the various
free churches. The Chapel of Unity is owned by them, but the
ground is leased by them from the Cathedral on a 999-year lease.
The idea of the Christian Service Centre has lapsed and in its
place is a hall *cum* refectory with kitchen and lavatories and with
a verger's flat above, which all now comes under the Cathedral.

APPENDIX B

Schedule of Requirements and Accommodation

The Cathedral

Competitors may place the new Cathedral anywhere within the boundary of the land edged red on the site plan. True west to east orientation is unessential. St. Michael's Avenue and the part of Priory Row which crosses the site may be built over if necessary.

The existing tower is to be retained, either separate or as part of the new Cathedral.

The two crypts indicated on the plan are of historic importance and must be retained, not necessarily within the confines of the new Cathedral but access to them from the Cathedral must be provided.

Note. The vaulting of the Crypts is near the floor level of the Cathedral, and important load-bearing walls or piers should avoid them as far as possible.

The old South Porch, with the Cappers Room over it which forms an interesting feature in Bayley Lane opposite the old St. Mary's Hall, may be retained and incorporated in the design of the New Cathedral at Competitors' discretion. (Bayley Lane need not be widened.)

The retention of any other part of the existing Cathedral is also left to the discretion of the Competitors.

Provision should be made in the Cathedral for the following forms of worship which will take place in it:

(a) The Daily Service of the Cathedral Clergy and Choir within the main Cathedral.

(*b*) The Sunday Services of a regular congregation of, say, 500 people.

(*c*) Large Diocesan or Civic Services.

(*d*) Festivals of Music.

The altar should be placed towards the 'East' in such a position that as many as possible of the congregation may have a clear and uninterrupted view. There should, therefore, be no screen for the chancel or choir 'West' of the altar.

There should be a throne for the Bishop and 24 stalls for the Provost, Chapter and Cathedral clergy.

The Cathedral should provide seating accommodation for 1250, amply spaced, exclusive of the Cathedral clergy and choir, with adequate room for liturgical movement. There should be additional permanent seating for 150 Diocesan clergy who may be present on great occasions, such seating being capable of use by the laity at other times. There should also be sufficient clear space in the body of the Cathedral so that an additional 250 chairs can be added when required.

The pulpit and lectern must each be given a position of importance and dignity in relation to the altar and congregation.

Provision should be made for a choir of 40 which, as far as possible, must not obscure the sight of the altar from the laity.

There should be a font which may be placed in a baptistry or in some other suitable position.

There should be a Lady Chapel to seat approximately 75.

There should be a Guild Chapel to seat 50, a Children's Chapel to seat 30, and a Chapel of the Resurrection for private prayer to seat 30.

Provision should be made inside the new Cathedral (possibly round the outer walls) for, say, eight 'Hallowing Places', each one symbolising the sacredness of one of the fields of activity which make

43. *The Lectern eagle modelled by Elizabeth Frink and cast in bronze.*

44. *The cluster of triads which are gathered to form a canopy over the Bishop's throne. Beyond to the right can be seen the golden light of the stained glass projected by the sun on to the white wall.*

45. *The Chapel of Christ in Gethsemane is for private prayer and meditation. It is screened off with a black steel Crown of Thorns designed by Basil Spence, who also designed the marble Altar. The relief mural is in ciment fondu by Steven Sykes. The Archangel is depicted with (right) the three sleeping disciples.*

up our daily human life (e.g. work, the arts, education, the home, commerce, healing, government, recreation). These 'Hallowing Places' could take the form of a shallow recess where a bas-relief sculpture or stained glass could represent the particular sphere of life and where visitors to the Cathedral could stand or kneel in prayer. Competitors are free to offer their own interpretation of this requirement.

Provision must be made for an organ which will be of Cathedral dimensions not necessarily placed in one position or unit.

It is desired that a place should be found in the precincts of the new Cathedral for the Charred Cross and Cross of Nails and also for the Altar of Rubble and the stones bearing the words 'Father Forgive'.

The layout of the ground round the Cathedral should make provision for an open-air pulpit and an open-air stage for religious plays.

The following ancillary accommodation is required:

(*a*) A Vestry for the Provost (to be used by the Bishop as required), with Secretary's room adjoining.

(*b*) A combined Chapter Meeting Room (i.e. Chapter House) and Canons' Vestry which will be used by 30 members of the Chapter.

(*c*) A large Choir Vestry and Choir Practice Room combined.

(*d*) A Sacristy.

(*e*) A Muniment Room (fire-resisting).

(*f*) A small preparation room for altar flowers.

(*g*) Proper storage accommodation.

Lavatory accommodation for (*a*) (*b*) (*c*) above, as well as limited facilities for the congregation.

Chapel of Unity

The Chapel of Unity will belong to the Joint Council of the Coventry Cathedral Christian Service Centre which is a separate body from the Cathedral Council and consists of members of the Church of England and the Free Churches. The chapel should be contiguous with the main Cathedral building, forming an integral part of the whole architectural grouping of the Cathedral, and having an important relationship to it. The position, shape and form of the chapel is left to the competitor. The chapel is to accommodate 200 persons. The chapel and the Cathedral should be divided by a vertical boundary plane for the purpose of indicating the distinction of ownership. The connection between the chapel and the Cathedral should be arranged so that worshippers in the chapel may, if so desired, feel themselves to be part of a Service taking place in the Cathedral, but also so that the chapel may be used independently of the Cathedral.

Christian Service Centre

The Christian Service Centre should form an architectural composition with the Cathedral but need not necessarily be attached to it.

The accommodation to be provided is as follows:

(*a*) A Meeting Room approximately 800 sq. ft. which could be used for meals.

(*b*) Suitable kitchen and service accommodation.

(*c*) One room 600 sq. ft. (available for Cathedral social purposes when required).

(*d*) Two rooms 400–500 sq. ft. (one to be used as a Reading Room).

(*e*) Two rooms for Administration, each 200 sq. ft.

(*f*) Lavatory accommodation for both sexes.

(*g*) Warden's Flat (Living Room, Study, Kitchen, 4 Bedrooms, Bathroon, etc.).

(*h*) Caretakers' accommodation (Living Room, Kitchen, 3 Bedrooms, Bathroom, etc.).

Appendix B

Provision should be made for the Christian Service Centre to be extended at some future date if found necessary.

Style and Materials

No restrictions are placed upon competitors as to style or materials to be used in any of the buildings. It is pointed out, however, that the existing Cathedral Tower and the nearby Holy Trinity Church, as well as the fourteenth/fifteenth-century St. Mary's Hall are all built in stone, and a similar good sandstone (light pink-grey in colour) is still available.

The photographs indicate the Georgian character of the houses facing Priory Row, which are to be retained, and the sketches are of the buildings to be erected in the new City.

Site Layout

In designing and estimating, competitors can ignore all graves and monuments inside and outside the existing Cathedral as to removal, replacement and cost which will be the responsibility of the Cathedral authorities.

Competitors are required to indicate their proposals for the layout of the whole of the site in addition to that covered by the Cathedral, Chapel of Unity and Christian Service Centre.

Competitors should bear in mind the necessity for proper means of access to the Cathedral and Chapel of Unity entrances (including vehicular access) and to the Christian Service Centre.

Provision for parking a limited number of cars (say 20) for officials should be arranged if possible. There will be a large public car park near the site.

Any of the trees on the site may be removed if found necessary, but the two shown on the plan are worth preserving if possible.

The line of Hill Top (an ancient Highway) leading in a northerly direction from Priory Row must be retained.

There must be provision in the layout for a Public Footway leading from West to East and finishing at Priory Street. This could be from Hill Top alongside or near the Northern boundary of the site.

Particulars of Drawings Required

All drawings to be in black ink or pencil on white paper (or black and white prints) with walls in plan and section filled in solid black or grey. Windows in elevations to be tinted light grey. No shades or shadows allowed in any of the drawings.

All drawings to be of double elephant size (40 × 27) and mounted on stiff boards without excess margins.

The following drawings are required:

Block plan to scale of 1/500.

Plans of the Cathedral, Chapel of Unity and Christian Service Centre to scale of 16 ft. to 1 inch.

Sufficient elevations and sections of all buildings adequately to illustrate the scheme, also to a scale of 16 ft. to 1 inch.

I sheet of ½-inch scale details of sufficient scope to illustrate the character of the design.

No perspective drawings allowed, but the successful Competitor will be required to provide a perspective after the award has been made.

The Chapel of Unity

The following notes are taken from suggestions made by the Joint Council of the Coventry Cathedral Christian Service Centre. They do not form part of the Conditions and Competitors are free to interpret the ideas expressed in whatever form they may think fit.

'The Chapel of Unity is probably the most difficult thing we set before the architect: we regard it as one of the most important. The

Chapel of Unity will belong both to the Free Churches and the Anglican Communion.

'We should wish to see it as an integral part of the whole architectural grouping of the Cathedral. It should not be seen as a secondary entity to be treated architecturally as an adjunct. It is essential in the thought as well as the structure of the Cathedral itself. We attach a fundamental spiritual importance to the Chapel of Unity within the Cathedral plan.

'We give the gist of discussion among ourselves that the imagination of the architect may play in the concrete and not within a vacuum. We have no wish to tie the imagination of the artist to any particular form, but we write what we have in our mind and leave the shaping of it to himself.

'The difficulties are great. First, the Chapel of Unity will be small in size, capable at most of seating 200 worshippers. The danger on the one hand is of its insignificance over against the mass of the Cathedral; on the other hand you will have a great building impressive in the unity of liturgical tradition, and therefore carrying its own message. How are we to find some comparable quality to hold the imagination in the smaller building? The Chapel of Unity must embody some form of sheer quality of its own to give it unique and comparable appeal.

'Functionally in architecture what does it stand for and what has it to say? We agree that we should think of it not only as an independent building; essentially it belongs within the Cathedral for some special purpose. The function we would give it is that of a place of intercession for the World Church. It will have two aspects—a looking outward now on to the World Church, and secondly a looking forward to unity.

'Furthermore the building will embody the thought of the descent of the Spirit upon the waiting Church. Liturgically it will have its centre in Pentecost, and will be the Chapel of Unity and of the Holy Spirit. That will give it a very specific function in perpetuity within the Cathedral and within its liturgical meaning.

'We are agreed that the shaping and the form of it be left to the architect, with the expression of our difficulties and needs and thoughts for his free imagination.'

APPENDIX C

The Architect's Report

COMPETITOR NO. 91
REPORT ON COVENTRY CATHEDRAL

1. *THE IDEA*

Through the ordeal of bombing, Coventry was given a beautiful ruin; the tower and spire reveal themselves for the first time in an arresting new aspect from the ruined nave. As the Cathedral stands now, it is an eloquent memorial to the courage of the people of Coventry. It is felt that the ruin should be preserved as a garden of rest, embracing the open-air pulpit and stage, and the new Cathedral should grow from the old and be incomplete without it.

The Altar

The altar is the heart of the new building; it can be seen from the ruined nave.

The Movable Glass Screens

The five glass screens dividing the porch from the nave are of clear glass, and, on great occasions and on warm summer evenings, can be lowered so that the Cathedral is open. There is no physical obstruction, on occasions such as these, between the whole population of Coventry and the altar.

The Right of Way

Saint Michael's Avenue, the traditional right of way, remains, except that it passes under the Cathedral porch within sight of the altar.

The Meaning of The Plan

As the life of Our Lord commenced with a star, the first element of the Cathedral plan is the Chapel of Unity, star-shaped, and is on the axis of the font. Then, turning towards the altar, the nave is flanked by the Hallowing Places and the windows shining towards the altar and representing the phases of life. This sequence culminates with the altar built by Mr. Forbes after the bombing of the Cathedral; it is surmounted by the charred cross, and backed by a great modern tapestry representing the crucifixion.

The Chapel of Unity

Much thought has been given to the position of the Chapel of Unity in the Cathedral plan. It must express Unity, and is the Chapel of the Holy Spirit; it has its place in Pentecost, and, if Baptists and Methodists are to worship according to their consciences and with sincerity, it may be wrong to be completely within sight of the altar. The Act of Baptism, however, is another matter, and, as unity is a primary consideration, the chapel is on the axis of the font. During combined Services, those wishing to be within sight of the altar can sit near the grille, which is the limit of the Chapel of Unity, though it must be stressed that the primary object in the design of this chapel is a room of prayer.

The chapel's shape represents Christian Unity; in elevation it is shaped like a Crusader's tent, as Christian Unity is a modern Crusade, and an attempt has been made to use dynamic crystalline forms which are contemporary, yet have their roots deep in the past.

The Font

The air breathed in the Cathedral is the same as in the Chapel of Unity, as no glass or solid material divides the chapel from the open nave; the legal division is represented by the open grille. Entering from the porch, the first important incident is the axis of the Chapel of Unity and the font. In the case of Coventry, the font has great significance; desire to perpetuate in the Church the youthful faith and courage of the people of Coventry can be expressed here. The font cover is conceived in a light steel sheet; a tall tapering form designed after the manner of a fir cone. The parts resembling ploughshares getting smaller as they near the point. Behind the font is the Baptistry window composed of 195 lights, 172 of which are of uniform size, and the stained-glass panels would not be too expensive as donations from the public.

The Hallowing Places

As suggested in the Conditions, the Hallowing Places are on the outer walls of the Cathedral. These are sculpted recesses with ideal lighting for bold relief.

The Stained-glass Windows

Great importance is given to the stained-glass windows; with the exception of the Baptistry windows and those lights over the entrance to the Chapel of Unity, all windows shine towards the altar. Behind the font the glass is very pale, almost white, with a slight tint of rose and pale blue, and, moving towards the altar, the next windows are composed in tones of green and yellow representing youth. The next pink and red, representing puberty, the next—the age of experience—are multi-coloured, then the age of wisdom—the windows are deep blue and purple—and, finally, the altar windows of golden glass. As in life, the colour of the windows is revealed only as you reach each stage—the past is known, the future is not. Only when the altar is reached the whole range of colour is seen for the first time.

The author of this design does not see this building as a planning problem, but the opportunity to create a Shrine to the Glory of God.

2. *THE PLAN*

The plan divides itself simply into four distinct elements: the old Cathedral, the Cathedral porch, the new Cathedral containing the Chapel of Unity, Guild Chapel, Lady Chapel, Children's Chapel, and the Chapel of the Resurrection, with all the attendant rooms, and finally, the Christian Service Centre Group, which includes the Warden's House and the Caretaker's House.

Vehicle access is centrally placed off Priory Row, and the service road leads from Priory Street to a yard which serves the Heating Chamber and all three kitchens (The Christian Service Centre, the Warden's kitchen and the Caretaker's Kitchen). Foot access to the Christian Service Centre is obtained from both the car park as well as Hill Top.

Access to the crypts is from under the Cathedral porch.

3. *GENERAL STRUCTURE*

Structurally, this building is planned on simple lines. A reinforced concrete vault, designed as lightly as possible, supported by tall elegant columns of steel cased in concrete, or post-stressed concrete units. Walls are of solid stone construction pierced with windows. The floor is concrete with a finished surface of patterned stone, and the foundations are of concrete.

(1) *The Vault*

It is proposed that the vaulting should be shell concrete approximately $2\frac{1}{2}''$ minimum thickness. Each vault to have reinforced concrete edge trimming beams for restraint, and these are to extend above the vault, and will constitute a grid of continuous beams extending from wall to wall and longitudinally down the building with point supports from columns.

The shuttering of the soffits is to be very carefully lined with narrow boarding to leave a regular and permanent pattern of board marking.

The infilling between ribs and over the vault is to be of Vermiculite screed (minimum depth $2''$) topped with $1\frac{1}{2}''$ of cement screed.

The roofing is of copper properly laid on roofing felt (if copper is available).

(2) *Columns*

It is hoped that it may be permissible to use a slenderness ration of not less than 200 in view of the support obtainable from the walls. Compound stanchions are proposed of heavily-plated cruciform sections to provide the required radius of gyration. Should it be necessary to work to a ratio of 150, the diameter of the columns—at present shown as $20''$ over all for a height of $60'$—will require to be somewhat increased. This would, of course, require to be the subject of detailed calculations. The compound stanchions would be completely encased (minimum cover $1\frac{1}{2}''$) in concrete of minimum test cube strength of 6,250 lbs. per square inch at 28 days, which should be compacted by external vibration.

It is proposed to re-use for all columns, in lifts of approximately $6'$, a standard metal drum shuttering faceted on the internal faces. The final column finish is to be bush hammering.

The use of column constructed of pre-case drums reinforced and stressed after erection has also been considered, but this required detailed analysis relative to the use of steel stanchions which would, at present, be premature.

(3) *Walls*

The slightly corrugated shape of the stone side walls, and their angled setting to the main roof vault in conjunction with the mesh of stone window heads and cills which connect the ends of bays produces an immensely strong saw-toothed wall in which the window sections tend to act as integral buttresses.

This wall provides maximum lateral support to the vault to meet both live and dead lateral loadings, and, in view of its strength, it may also be used to relieve the columns of a proportion of the vertical roof component through the grid of continuous beams, thus permitting a relatively light column section to be used.

Type of Stone

It was considered essential that the same stone, or a similar variety to that of the old Cathedral, be used. Where possible, mouldings and other expensive masons' carvings, have been eliminated. Simple chamfors are used, and decoration is in the form of sculpture which is not much more expensive than an elaborately moulded wall surface carried out by masons. This stone is used for the Christian Service Centre as well.

The walling below the main floor level, as appears on both east and west elevation, is in grey granite blocks backed by brick. On the west elevation, this embraces the Choir Vestry, and ceases where it joins the Warden's House. On the east elevation, it butts on to the Guild Chapel corridor.

(4) *The Floor*

The floor slab carried the heating elements. The finished surface is composed of a pattern of stone slabs of varying cool colours to contrast with the pinkey-grey walls. Under the porch, however, cobbles are interspersed with stone slabs to catch surface water which may permeate from the outside.

(5) Foundations

Foundations are normal, being constructed of concrete.

4. *DETAILED DESCRIPTION*

(1) *The Old Cathedral*

In order to establish which parts of the Cathedral can be left standing a detailed examination will be required. It is the intention to preserve as much of the old as possible, and it will be necessary to protect the upper surfaces by some method of damp-proofing (preferably lead if obtainable) to prevent deterioration through the years. The old Cathedral should then be planted out with trees, shrubs, and flowers, and certain creepers should be encouraged to grow over the old walls, and the large paved area adjacent to the porch would serve for the congregation during open-air Services.

A cross of English oak replaces the charred cross, and a new altar of grey granite replaces Mr. Forbes' altar. The pulpit and canopy are of concrete with exposed aggregate.

The open-air stage is unaltered from its existing position, as this has the ideal orientation, and gives an excellent setting for religious plays.

(2) *The Porch*

The porch grows from the old Cathedral, and it has been designed in the lightest and most unobtrusive way as an introduction to the new building. The spacing of the five bays which form the mathematical unit on which the whole plan has been designed are taken from the old Cathedral.

Vault and Columns. The concrete groined vault is supported on concrete pillars which are clothed in stone. Access to the crypts is from the south-west corner of the porch.

(3) *The Nave, Choir and Aisles*

The Glass Screens. The five glass screens dividing the porch from the nave are capable of being lowered into the floor. This has been done successfully in the Crematorium at Stockholm, and assurance has been given by engineers here that this is not a difficult task, and relatively low power is required to lower and raise these screens by the careful use of counter-balanced weights. Each screen has a set of doors which come into operation when the screens are in the raised position.

Seating. The nave accommodates the seating. The area indicated on the plan is the extent of the heated floor slab. The total number of chairs accommodated on this slab is 1,374 and, as the aisles are 18′ wide, there should be no difficulty in adding the 250 extra seats asked for in the conditions; a method has been shown on the main plan. The spacing for the chairs has been taken as 2′ 10″ back to back by 1′ 8″ wide.

Choir Stalls. The choir stalls are designed to accommodate 40 choir and an organist and console; on the opposite side, stalls for 24 clergy and a bishop's throne. They are constructed in laminated wood moulded to shape, and the ornamented areas are fretted out and carved by hand. Brass fittings are introduced as connections. These should not be brightly finished but have a protective dull finish.

Pulpit and Lectern. Looking towards the altar, the pulpit is on the left and the lectern on the right. The pulpit is constructed of Portland stone with a laminated wood sounding board designed to be acoustically correct. The lectern is the traditional brass eagle.

The Bishop's Throne. The Bishop's throne is designed for fabric, probably a brocade, cobalt blue in colour, and the details of the embroidery are shown on the half-inch detail.

The Altar. As already mentioned, the altar is the existing one which is carried into the Cathedral along with the charred cross and the cross of nails, as relics.

The Tapestry. The tapestry is backed by a stone wall, and is hanging from great bronze pins built into the wall. This tapestry, for which £30,000 has been allowed in the estimate, could be designed by a great contemporary artist, or a competition might be organised and the firm who exhibited modern tapestries in the recent Arts Council Exhibition in London have been approached, and have the necessary scope to undertake this commission. This would be the largest tapestry in the world, and would be the most beautiful background for the altar and the charred cross. The subject of the tapestry is the Crucifixion.

The Hallowing Places. Ten Hallowing Places are shown on the plan, each one is a sculptured recess, but the stained-glass windows, casting their different colours over the sculpture, would make them slightly different from each other. An altar slab is included on each Hallowing Place for the placing of flowers.

Space for Organ. Space for the organ is allowed for over the ways to the Children's Chapel and the Chapel of the Resurrection.

(4) *The Chapel of Unity*

The Chapel of Unity is simply constructed on a concrete foundation with large diamond-shaped mullions of stone which support the roof of concrete. Attention is drawn to the fact that the floor is slightly dished, and the star pattern should be of golden stone and the remaining infilling of blue marble. The central symbol of the Holy Spirit is of mosaic.

Vestry. A small vestry has been incorporated within the boundaries of the Chapel of Unity, and this is provided with a small cupboard and a lavatory.

(5) *The Children's Chapel*

To create the correct atmosphere for the children the wrought iron screen in the Children's Chapel, which is detailed on $\frac{1}{2}''$, is composed of a pattern of flowers and animals, and, above the transome, the firmaments, with the Virgin Mary and the Infant Christ set in an area of golden stars. The chapel itself may be decorated with a mural in a simple understanding technique. This chapel seats 30.

(6) *The Lady Chapel*

The Lady Chapel, which seats 70, is placed in its traditional position behind the altar, and the large window which is shown on the north elevation, lights the interior. The walls are of stone, and the roof of deep concrete beams which should be brightly coloured in rich mediaeval colours of green, red, white, black and gold. Adjacent to the chapel is a small room for the preparation of altar flowers.

(7) *The Chapel of the Resurrection*

The Chapel of the Resurrection balances the Children's Chapel, and seats 30. Behind the altar is an incised carving on Portland stone developing the idea of the three crosses which are in the existing Chapel of the Resurrection.

(8) *The Guild Chapel*

The Guild Chapel, which can accommodate 80 people, gets its character from the tall mullioned walls. A feature of this design is that the windows can represent all the trades, and the stained-glass designs can incorporate the arms of the various guilds.

(9) *Lower Ground Floor*

Provost's Vestry. The lower ground floor is designed as a working adjunct to the main Cathedral above. It accommodates the Chapter

House, the Provost's Vestry and his Secretary, the Muniment Room and the Sacristy, the Choir Vestry, which is provided with lockers on one end wall, and also with the necessary cloaks and lavatories. A large assembly area is also provided. The Provost's Vestry has an excellent outlook towards the new City Library and Art Gallery, and has a south-easterly aspect. The Secretary's room is conveniently placed in relation to the Provost's Vestry; a small cloakroom and lavatory are provided.

Chapter House. The Chapter House is designed to accommodate 30 members of the Chapter, seats being provided correctly uphol-stered, in the window recesses. 37 recesses are shown on the plan.

Muniment Room and Sacristy. The Muniment Room is of fireproof construction. The exact requirements of the Muniment Room and Sacristy are not stated in the conditions, but attention is drawn to the fact that this part of the plan is flexible, and allows of latitude in design and any special requirements within reason can be provided once these are known.

Access. Entrances to the lower ground floor are by two doors—one from the east and the other from the west. The eastern door is marked on the plan as Canon's door; the western door is shown as the Choir door.

Staircase. Access to the main Cathedral floor is by a staircase which is 4' 6" wide and 3 landings are provided; the tread is 10" and the rise 6".

(10) *Cathedral Storage*

Provision has been made on the lower ground floor on the east side of the Cathedral for the storage of chairs; access from the Cathedral is obtained by a small stair, and also by a lift. The lift is a goods type, which is intended for the movement of furniture, etc.

(11) *The Christian Service Centre*

This group embraces the Warden's House, the Caretaker's House, and the Christian Service Centre itself. An attempt has been made to create a building of friendly secluded and domestic character which people would enjoy using, and make a habit of visiting. The position was considered carefully, as it allows of future extension on to the spare ground to the extreme north-west of the Cathedral site. It groups happily with No. 11 Priory Row, which is a beautiful building, and which is to be restored and brought into the Cathedral plan. A suggestion is shown on the main plan as to how this building could group with the Christian Service Centre. The car park is convenient, and an intimate foot approach can be made through Hill Top.

The building is planned so that all the kitchens face on to the yard, the main kitchen serving the Meeting Room, the Warden's Kitchen and also the Caretaker's Kitchen.

The Warden's House. The Warden's House has been planned as an integral part of the Christian Service Centre, but his house is conveniently placed in relation to Cathedral. The accommodation asked for has been provided, and the total area of the house is 1,760 sq. ft. The Warden has direct access to the Christian Service Centre.

Caretaker's House and the Kitchen. The caretaker, who, it is understood, is to control the feeding arrangements, has his 1,300 sq. ft. flat over the main Meeting Room. He has direct access to the main kitchen, which has been shown small and easy to run with a small staff, as it is assumed that light snacks and teas will be the type of meal provided. It is possible, however, to provide a larger kitchen on a lower level, using the existing one as a Servery, if this is thought necessary.

Appendix C

(12) *Christian Service Centre Group*

Meeting Room. The Meeting Room occupies a central position on the plan, and overlooks a garden and a pool through a verandah which faces due south. There is a small entrance hall with a staircase feeding the cloakroom at half basement level.

Social Room. The upper floors are occupied by a Social Room and two other rooms asked for in the conditions.

Reading Room. The Reading Room is placed on the end of the circulation, with a southern balcony for those wishing peace and quiet.

Administration. Two administrative rooms are placed off the entrance hall.

5. *HEATING AND LIGHTING*

Heating

It is proposed to use an accelerated low-pressure hot water system with floor coils set in the floor slab. These will be divided into approximately 5 separate sections for control purposes.

It has been decided to use the building fabric, and particularly the heavy slab floor, for thermal storage, thus eliminating the expense of and the space required for thermal storage tanks, etc.

Calculations indicate that a temperature drop of not more than 1° per hour can be expected once the heating is turned off, and it is, therefore, practicable to run the boilers during the off-peak period only when advantage can be taken of the cheaper rates and the certainty of supply.

Present costs indicate that gas-fired boilers will be the most economical, and especially so if cheap off-peak rates now under discussion become available. Should electricity become an economical proposition while the Cathedral is being built, this method of heating can readily be installed, using electrode boilers in preference to gas-fired ones. The lower ground floor and the Christian Service Centres are heated by low-pressure radiators off the same system.

The position of the gas flue is shown on plan, and the fumes are dispersed from an opening behind the parapet at roof level.

Lighting

Straightforward tungsten lighting is suggested. The type of fitting is indicated on the half-inch detail—the only departure from this method is the illumination of the tapestry, which should be discreetly floodlit.

6. ESTIMATE OF COST

In order to arrive at a cube, quantities were taken out and priced at the rates current as at 30th October 1950. In a building such as this, it is impossible to guess a cube, and the reinforced concrete vault, the stone work, floor slab and heating, the furnishing of the Cathedral, and also its decoration, were all accounted for in arriving at a cube figure. The only part that has been cubed without quantities is the Christian Service Centre and the one-story link with the Cathedral. The sum of £30,000 is allowed for the great tapestry, and a contingency sum of £10,000 has also been provided for.

Cube rate Cost

Cubing at 5s. 6d. for the main Cathedral, and 5s. 4d. for the Christian Service Centre, the cost is estimated at £801,103 16s. 4d. (eight hundred and one thousand, one hundred and three pounds, sixteen shillings and fourpence stg.); this excludes the cost of the organ and the cost of the layout. It does include, however, for the terrace, the paving in the porch, and the steps leading to the old Cathedral, and the formation of the new walls which form part of the old Cathedral.

APPENDIX D

Report by Assessors to the Chairman
and Members of the Coventry Cathedral
Reconstruction Committee

We have examined the 219 designs which have been submitted in this Competition. Although we consider the general level of the designs is disappointing, yet we are very happy to report our conviction that the Competition has succeeded in bringing forth several designs of great merit, and one of outstanding excellence.

We make our award as follows:

> First Premium to Design No. 91.
> Second Premium to Design No. 202.
> Third Premium to Design No. 11.

Design No. 91. In selecting this design we not only feel that it is the best design submitted, but that it is one which shows that the Author has qualities of spirit and imagination of the highest order. He lets the Conditions grow under his hand to produce a splendid Cathedral, and as the Conditions are unusual, the resulting conception is unusual; revealing the author's ability to solve the problem of designing a Cathedral in terms of contemporary architecture.

The Author in his Report stresses the beauty of the existing destroyed Cathedral as an eloquent memorial to the courage of the people of Coventry, and states it as his opinion that the major part of it should be allowed to stand as a Garden of Rest, treating it as an Atrium to the New Cathedral which 'should grow out of the old Cathedral and be incomplete without it'.

The interior fully meets the requirements of liturgical movement. The Altar is not narrowly confined within the usual Chancel but is open on its sides to the full width of the Nave. The Hallowing Places are admirably treated, being recesses canted toward the congregation from the wide passage aisles with lighting which falls only from the side onto beautifully designed Sculpture appropriate to each Hallowing Place, avoiding all glare to the eyes.

The Chapel of Unity is not a mere adjunct to the Cathedral but a Building elemental in form and of great significance. It is independent of, yet an integral part of, the Cathedral; separated from the Nave only by an open metal Screen. The Author strongly advocates that this Chapel should have its axis on the Font and this is what he has devised, making the Font in the Cathedral of special importance.

The shape of the new Cathedral is impressively simple, the existing Tower being an essential part of the Design.

The vaulting of the interior is of reinforced concrete; the walls externally and internally are of pink-grey stone.

The Half Inch Details show that the Author is capable of most skilled and sensitive design.

The Chapter House, the Christian Service Centre, Warden's and Caretaker's Houses, have much architectural merit, in keeping with the Cathedral itself.

The Estimate of Cost, clearly set out in the able Report, is in our opinion reasonable.

Design No. 202 provides a very convincing solution to the problem of lay-out and the grouping of the various elements of the design. The existing Tower and portions of the ruined Cathedral are incorporated into a Cloister of considerable charm, integrated with the new Cathedral.

Appendix D

This also is a design contemporary in character which has unusual qualities of simplicity and distinction.

The drawings, particularly the half inch details, suggest that the Author has not fully developed the basic potentialities of his design. Nevertheless, it is well worthy of second place.

Design No. 11 is a competent and well-thought-out scheme, with a lay-out somewhat similar to that of the second premiated design. The plan and composition of the masses are impressive, but the design lacks distinction in quality of architectural detail.

Apart from the premiated designs there are two to which we wish to accord Special Mention, No. 128 and No. 8.

Design No. 128 is of great merit with an inspiring interior, and an original and interesting conception of structure. Unfortunately a failure adequately to comply with certain of the planning conditions precludes it from being considered for an Award.

Design No. 8 is a well-devised scheme, carefully worked out in detail with attractive features, but lacks that architectural character and atmosphere essential to a Cathedral.

Among the remainder, Nos. 81, 111, 114, 125, 141, 173 and 174 all exhibit considerable merit and present special points of interest; but it is evident that the majority of competitors found the problem a difficult one, and a large number failed to appreciate the requirements. Many were able to produce satisfactory plans, but few were able to build these up to form satisfactory cathedrals.

PERCY THOMAS
EDWARD MAUFE
HOWARD ROBERTSON

Index

Italic figures indicate the preceding text page facing plates

Index

Italic figures indicate the preceding text page facing plates

Italic figures indicate the preceding text page facing plates

Index

Italic figures indicate the preceding text page facing plates

Italic figures indicate the preceding text page facing plates

Italic figures indicate the preceding text page facing plates

Italic figures indicate the preceding text page facing plates